ACKNOWLEDGEMENTS

The process of writing a fun and engaging literary journey about the craft beer business has been a total blast! I could not have completed **Occupation Fermentation** without invaluable support from a broad range of family, friends, advisors and industry colleagues along the way.

I want to give a special shout out to the numerous craft brewers across the US that I have chatted with during my time researching this book. They have graciously given of their precious time, shared many fun anecdotes and provided a special window into their recipes for success. I had the difficult task of choosing among the various "stories of triumph" to illustrate the many diverse ways to build a successful craft business.

I would especially like to thank **Tim Klatt** of Strange Land Brewery in Austin (TX), **Jeff Browning** of Brewport Brewing Co. in Bridgeport (CT) and **Mike Bristol** of Bristol Brewing Company in Colorado Springs (CO). All are seasoned brew masters and entrepreneurs that spent extensive time sharing their perspective on the history, joys and challenges of our rapidly evolving craft industry.

I must recognize **Gary Breitbart** who graciously listened to my ideas and provided invaluable feedback to improve the content. I had tremendous assistance and guidance in designing, organizing and editing this book from **Rick Glover**, a true branding and marketing whiz. In addition, **Martha Beale** provided that special inspiration through extensive brainstorming of book names.

Nobody has been more crucial to me in the pursuit of this project than my family. Most importantly, I wish to thank my loving wife **Sheryl** whom has been a positive and encouraging voice since I first shared my vision for this project.

Finally, I recognize my daughter **Kendall** for her never ending belief that anything can be accomplished in life by always striving for success and overcoming those many obstacles that will arise.

Occupation Fermentation

Table of Contents

PREFACE

I remember when that first dream of my life's mission came into focus.   It was back in high school.

It all started when I took an introductory cooking class and learned the basic elements of putting together a great meal.   I began making simple dishes like scrambled eggs, French toast, omelets and pancakes.   Gradually, I broadened my capabilities to include soups, sandwiches and stews.   Ultimately, I became skilled enough to make dinner for our family

I expanded this focus to helping around the house when my folks entertained friends and business colleagues. I served as the Sous Chef helping prepare various main courses and side dishes at many elaborate dinner parties. I very much enjoyed my time in the kitchen which made me wonder what type of career would allow me to further my interest in gourmet food preparation and all its elements.

I secured a part-time job at a local three star restaurant working my way up in more demanding roles. I started as a dishwasher, then moved to busboy, and eventually expanded to cold food preparation. I even helped with cooking the Inn's famous Sunday brunch.

The owner, a graduate of the School of Hotel Administration at Cornell University, encouraged me to pursue a career in the hospitality business. I applied to Cornell and was accepted as a full-time student.

During my four years I learned all facets of hotel, club, bar and restaurant operations. A course that held a particular interest was named Introduction to Wines & Spirits. This is where I received my first dedicated exposure to fine wines, beers and spirits, from around the world.

While at Cornell, I received significant "hands-on" experience during summer and work-study programs with Sheraton Hotels, Walt Disney World and American Airlines.

I was exposed to all facets of the hospitality industry, while developing a further appreciation of the nuances of running a successful business. I also was determined to maintain a connection to my "foodie" nature no matter where my career and life experience might lead.

Upon graduation from Cornell I secured my first job working at a golf resort in Florida. I had the opportunity to put into practice all the book learning I had experienced during my college days. This was the lead in to my first management gig with a major hotel company - Guest Quarters (now Doubletree Hotels). I assumed a variety of roles ranging from overseeing the front office to having full control of the property during night and weekend hours.

My long-term goal was to build the skills needed to ultimately to create and operate my own enterprise. I have been blessed with an extensive corporate career with both the Pepsi-Cola Company (beverages) and Jones Lang LaSalle (real estate). My primary focus was in finance, strategy and operational excellence during my tenure with these industry leaders. Whether it was helping create a new soft drink category or finding space for a new restaurant venture, I have stayed engaged with current trends over the years.

This experience was especially valuable when I helped lead two high profile real estate projects in New York City. First, I was actively involved in the redevelopment of Grand Central Terminal into a dynamic food, entertainment and shopping mecca. Second, I assisted in the planning and reimagining of the World Trade Center Site after the terrorist attacks of 9/11.

I helped determine the optimal mix of restaurants, cafes, boutique shops, quick dining options and luxury brands creating a new global tourist destination in lower Manhattan. These two assignments have enhanced my ability to take a team's vision and transform it into a working enterprise under constantly changing conditions.

More recently, I have transitioned to being an entrepreneur and advising a variety of early-stage and developing companies across a broad range of industries. The common theme I encounter is how to convert a simple idea into a business that can grow profitably and last the test of time.

I have stayed in touch with many of my hotelie friends over the years as our careers have grown and changed. As such, I have followed closely the rapid growth and evolution going on in the craft brewing space. Recently, I worked with several regional brewers that are carving out unique niches in this rapidly changing industry.

My experience has highlighted the fact that just brewing a great product is only the first step to being successful. I find that it is even more critical to understand the core concepts of marketing, operations, capital raising and financial management.

I decided that I would share my depth of experience through a new venture (CraftBeerInsights.com) that services brewers of all sizes across the USA.

Occupation Fermentation opens the reader's eyes to the challenges and rewards of being in the craft brewing business. You will find it a fun and easy read that provides valuable information on all elements of building a successful and profitable craft brewery.

I look forward to connecting with you in the near future. Please feel free to reach out with any comments and call if I can be of assistance to you as you grow your venture.

I offer a free 30-minute consultation for those forward-looking owners, investors and operators aiming to quickly generate more cash flow from their enterprises. It is always an enjoyable experience for me to speak with you, the reader of Occupation Fermentation, about all aspects of your business. And it's a real treat for me to gain new friends in the process and learn from you at the same time!

Curt Battles
September 2018

INTRODUCTION

What do a Pink Flamingo, the Ivywild School, Hopping Gnomes and a Funky Buddha have in common? They are just a sampling of the unique stories and names that I have encountered while putting together this book on the Craft Brewing Industry. With its promise of innovative brews, and a "cool" factor to share amongst friends, it seems that all kinds of folks want to jump into this hyper competitive business.

Once you have perfected the optimum juicy IPA, how do you actually build a profitable business? No doubt, many of you may want to brag about being a brewery owner and at each step want to make informed decisions. That insures you can achieve the success you seek thorough an understanding of all business aspects, from operations through marketing and distribution, that are critical to that success.

Occupation Fermentation is all about teaching the core concepts needed to build a sustainable, successful craft beer business. I will touch on a variety of critical subjects including how to name your brewery and beers (e.g. marketing), what makes the craft beer business hot (e.g. history and competitive profile) and paying for your dream (e.g. raising money). Whether the goal is to have a brewpub that serves the local market or to become a regional juggernaut with production in excess of 15,000 barrels, it all begins at the same place.

Let's get started with a brief story that will help put your quest in perspective. Recently, I spoke with Mike Bristol at Bristol Brewing Company, who has been brewing beer for nearly 25 years. I asked him how and why he got started on this journey.

Back in 1994, Mike and his wife Amanda settled comfortably in Colorado Springs and started hand-brewing fresh, distinctive ales for the locals. Mike is a Mechanical Engineer by training, and found that his occupation was somewhat uninspiring following his first gig after college working for Nissan Automotive.

He developed a love for making beer through homebrewing on a small rig, but had never thought about doing it for a living. That soon changed when he started building his own equipment. "I fell in love with the process, the romance, and the history," says Bristol.

Watching other small craft brewers in his hometown of Fort Collins triggered the revelation that this might indeed be his calling. In fact, at the beginning Mike connected with some of the local pioneers in craft beer (Odell Brewing Company & New Belgium Brewing) to better understand how best to proceed in starting a real business. Back in those days he was a visionary on the forefront of the fledgling craft beer industry.

His business has consistently grown over time, so Bristol now produces over 13,000 barrels (or approximately 180,000 cases of beer) annually as a large micro brewer. Nevertheless, he continues to be locally focused with no distribution outside the state of Colorado. Mike cites a number of reasons for staying in-state… it's a lot easier and better for the beer, he wanted to be the local brewery, it establishes a connection with the community and preserves a family oriented environment. His perspective is that "you just have to own your backyard otherwise you will not see a long-term play" for the business.

In 2013, Bristol moved its entire brewery operation into a newly renovated former elementary school (Ivywild). The brewery continues its fiercely local focus with a community-oriented facility that includes a bakery, a coffee roaster/cafe, a distilled spirits bar and an all-purpose meeting room. This innovative location allows the Bristol team to stay actively engaged with the community on a daily basis. Mike stated that "it's not easy to translate that value outside your core market" as a further reason for their winning strategy.

Here the team, happily ignore school rules by brewing and serving beer in the classrooms, including the onsite brew pub. Built in 1916, the building's hardwood floors and brick walls, former gym and student artwork radiate charm and a hip but super-friendly vibe.

Ultimately the $5.0 MM expansion provided the needed capacity for growing demand and allows the brew masters to continually create new specialty beers. A really cool thing about Bristol is its focus on giving back to the community. Mike indicated that it is by design that Bristol's award-winning beers remain available only in Colorado.

He and his team believe in local breweries and in their ability to build community. "The ability to focus on serving the people who live, work, and play side by side with us is critical", Mike said. "In fact, the Community Ales program (unique beers for non-profit groups) alone generates hundreds of thousands of dollars for worthy causes within our community annually".

Another thing that hasn't changed about Bristol: Even in this era of the hoppy beer, the brewery's best seller remains Laughing Lab, a malty Scottish ale. The beer has won nine Great American Beer Festival Awards since 1994, including two golds. That, not surprisingly, was the first beer brewed in the new location. Ultimately, Mike said a brewer's task is to "make the best quality product possible" and "be authentic about who you are as a brewery".

So what is the first lesson you will take away from this amazing tale is how each of the breweries and founding entrepreneurs throughout the book had a clear vision on what they wanted to achieve. It shows there are many ways to measure success in the fun and changing craft brewing business. It could be the quality of the brews as measured by gold medals or focusing solely on being the clear leader in their local marketplace. Alternatively, it may be a focus on being sold across the country in every state. In all cases, it requires building a business that actual turns a consistent profit and can help fund the new equipment often required with rapid expansion.

The ideas and concepts you will learn in this book are designed to be entertaining, enlightening and practical at the same time. I hope you will enjoy diving into chapters about creating a brand with the same gusto as figuring out the right size brewing system for your business. In fact, you can use this as a "roadmap" for charting out how to organize your enterprise for success, all the while having a great time doing it. Cheers and best of luck with your brewing endeavors!

Chapter One

Do You Have the Right Stuff to Succeed?

I know you are a huge fan of all types of craft beer (especially since you are reading this book)! It could be you thirst for a juicy hop forward I.P.A. or that special Brown Lager available only in a vibrant tasting room. This passionate interest has led you to travel "far and wide" to find the latest and greatest award winning brews. How often have you found yourself (and hundreds of other craft lovers) "queued up" in a line that snakes several blocks around a brewery at 1 AM? The thrill of being the first to secure a precious six-pack of that limited release special addition ale is an amazing feeling. In fact, you are so fanatical about your favorite brew that you really do not want to drink anything else.

This craft beer fervor may well have led you to create your own unique lagers as an aspiring home brewer in the basement or garage. No doubt, it was quite a challenge figuring out the equipment needed, getting everything properly assembled and then running the brewing system for the first time.

It probably has taken months of trial and error to finally bring forth the fruits of your labors to share with family and friends to rave reviews. Moreover, while tinkering with the various recipes for an American blonde ale or German Weiss bier you had a magical moment.

Sitting around with your buddies and enjoying a fabulous new beer a wonderful idea crossed your mind: **I should open my own brewery, make some money and have this much fun everyday!**

This chapter offers my viewpoint on the unique challenges that you will encounter as an entrepreneur. It provides an overview of the positives and negatives that you will experience as you start and grow a profitable craft brewing empire. These same lessons apply whether you are servicing only your local pub or overseeing a major regional brewer.

It also highlights how to successfully make the transition from a worker bee to an owner mentality. Most importantly, it helps in identifying whether you indeed have the "right stuff" to ultimately be successful

!

What is Entrepreneurship?

Here are a few questions for you to consider when contemplating starting your own enterprise.

- *Do you have any idea how to create a brand name for your amazing beers that is unique and distinctive?*

- *Can you identify those financial sources that will provide immediate and on-going support to get your dream microbrewery up and running?*

- *What impact will having a vibrant tasting room experience have on your ability to draw new true believers every week?*

- *How will you feel when making the weekly payroll becomes a major struggle?*

- *Have you ever managed a team of individuals to achieve a common goal especially with limited resources?*

I suspect that most of you have either previously worked within a large corporation or even at a local business. The role you filled may have been in sales, marketing, day-to-day operations or even accounting. It certainly was great to have a steady gig and receive a paycheck every two weeks. Yet, it seemed there was a key portion of your talents going to waste as you went about the daily grind.

It often seemed that there were too many constraints placed upon your creativity and when you had a brilliant idea it did not seem to be recognized or appreciated. In addition, there was a series of endless meetings and discussions just to make a decision on the simplest of issues (e.g. changing the type of coffee in the break room).

In fact, you may have thought many times "I would do this completely differently if this were my company". So now you are seriously thinking that it would be great to truly control your destiny by become your own boss. This is a major first step on the way to starting your own enterprise and becoming an entrepreneur. Yet, it is more than a simple notion to transfer that passion for making fine beers into becoming a successful business owner.

There are many examples of this enduring can do spirit in numerous technology startups that impact our daily life. Some intriguing ideas that are disrupting old ways of thinking include Flipboard, Google, Amazon, Uber, SnapChat, Instagram, Airbnb and Tesla. Entrepreneurs searching for a better way and fed up with business as usual have launched these firms that fulfill consumer's demands.

This search for the next big thing reminds me of a quote from the famous poet Maya Angelou - **"My mission in life is not merely to survive, but to thrive; and to do so with some passion, some compassion, some humor, and some style"**.[1]

I think this sentiment captures the entrepreneurial spirit to both think outside of the box and be willing to dream big.

A new report from the Global Entrepreneurship Monitor (GEM), sponsored by Babson College and Baruch College, finds that of 27 million working-age Americans--nearly 14 percent--are starting or running new businesses. That's a record high for this study, now in its 16th year. And it's an impressive showing for a developed economy, where finding work with an employer is easier

---

[1] Brainy Quotes: Maya Angelou - *brainyquote.com*

and capturing market share harder than in less-developed nations.[2]

The GEM study showed that a growing number of people consider entrepreneurship an attractive career option. Fifty-one percent of the working population believes good opportunities exist for starting businesses, the first time that figure has risen above half. Better yet, 80 percent of those who plan to start businesses in the next three years are doing something about it, such as leasing space, refining business plans or registering their companies.

I did a quick Google search and found this nice summary from Dictionary.com:

> **"A person who organizes and manages any enterprise, especially a business, usually with considerable initiative and risk."**

Now that you have the basic concept a few questions may naturally pop into your mind.

- Do you start to wonder whether *entrepreneur* simply means "a person who starts a business and is willing to risk loss in order to make money"?

- Can it also carry the additional meaning of a person with far-sightedness and desire to innovate?

---

[2] The U.S. Now Has 27 Million Entrepreneurs - Leigh Buchanan; *Inc.*, September

The answer, perhaps to no one's surprise, is that the role of entrepreneur can and should go in both directions. I actually think a great way to get a sense of what managing an enterprise means is best illustrated by various legends in their respective fields. I have found some quotes that really speak to the ingenuity, determination, wisdom, free spirit and planning needed to become a business leader!

- "Success is not the key to happiness. Happiness is the key to success. If you love what you are doing, you will be successful." - *Albert Schweitzer*

- "Ideas are easy. Implementation is hard." - Guy Kawasaki

- "Do not be embarrassed by your failures, learn from them and start again." - Richard Branson

- "I'm convinced that about half of what separates the successful entrepreneurs from the non-successful ones is pure perseverance." - Steve Jobs

- "If you're not a risk taker, you should get the hell out of business." - Ray Kroc

I encourage you to do some deep thinking, usually over a great Session IPA, to determine if this should be your future professional pathway. Becoming an entrepreneur can be an amazing journey if you have a healthy tolerance for risk taking. The entrepreneurial pathway often requires a constant change in plans and early disappointments can lead to great finishes and long-term success.

How Do I Know If I Am Ready?

Now lets consider those special qualities that make a successful business leader and how you can assess your readiness. You will notice that I am continually pointing out follow your passion and do what you love it makes the long hours and various sacrifices encountered along the way well worth the effort.

Right now, we are seeing a dynamic reordering of the global economy that I am convinced requires a seismic shift in the way that we, as individuals, view and manage our skills set. In other words, each of you brings talents, experiences, perspectives and connections into the workplace that are shared with an employer in exchange for guaranteed salary, benefits and other forms of compensation.

In fact, everyone starts from a different place – from recent graduates to established professionals looking for a new direction; from those early in their career looking for the next step to aspiring home brewers looking for their big break. Now is an ideal moment to reflect about your current career and desired future direction. No matter where you are on the journey, let's energize your thinking about how to follow your dreams.

I have recently reimagined my own future, and made this shift, starting a craft brewing consulting practice (Craft Beer Insights). I have labored for more than 25 years in corporate America in the three major industries;

Hospitality, Beverage and Commercial Real Estate. During that time I helped lead two iconic redevelopment projects -- Grand Central Terminal and the World Trade Center (post 9/11) in NYC.

I developed a broad financial, marketing and operational skill set, learned to navigate intense political environments, charted long term strategic direction and experienced tremendous personal growth. These various professional experiences augment the core abilities that I use everyday to grow my entrepreneurial dreams. I bring that special focus in helping growing craft brewers fine tune their operations to ultimately become profitable.

Two Key Steps to Entrepreneurial Success

Over time I became increasingly frustrated with laboring for others, and dreamed of having my own enterprise in order to get added flexibility, a stimulating learning environment and the potential for financial freedom.

Thus, I entered the world of entrepreneurship. That is part of the reason that becoming your own boss can be both exhilarating and downright scary at the same time! It is very much like the scene in a favorite movie of mine: "Indiana Jones and The Last Crusade." Indy must cross a wide chasm when there is no apparent bridge or pathway. Only by taking a leap of faith does he succeed. Once he takes his first step, a stone pathway appears, providing him access to the other side where he can once again, save the day.

The entrepreneurial life is a total blast if you are comfortable managing an ever-changing landscape and perpetual uncertainty, often involving your near-term financial well-being. Over the past few years, I have learned to overcome my concerns and embrace the adventure. It takes time and a strong sense of self to conquer fears – you need faith, confidence in yourself, and unending hard work. Here are two key lessons I have learned along the way that should help smooth your path forward.

First, have the courage to Dream Big – Now, more than ever, I believe "if you can dream it, you can achieve it." I was attending a conference a few years ago where I met the riveting speaker -- Robert Moss, who wrote the book, **"The Three Only Things"**. His book gave numerous examples of how dreams help individuals open up wells of possibilities and escape self-limiting beliefs and behaviors by bringing the subconscious into the light of day. He contends that dreams are in fact, "not on our case -- they are on our side," as they show us things we might not want to think about, but could actually benefit from, if we remain open to them.

The chance for you to impact this type of positive change for people in need is one source of inspiration. The revelation that I could combine my "passion" and earn a respectable living on my own terms became the basis for my new firm.

Second as an entrepreneur you need to Take Care of Number One and Build in Personal Recovery Time. When you're out on your own, there are significant temptations to work 24/7 on your new enterprise. There is an inherent danger of early burnout and strategic errors from not taking the time to sit back and reflect on your efforts each day. While initial concepts and gut feelings derived from a conversation or interaction may be correct, decisions made when you are hot versus cool can often be wrong.

I have found that when I actually sleep on an idea overnight, I reach a more well thought out series of alternative approaches by letting a bit of time pass. I awake with clarity and the ability to chart a clear path forward with confidence.

This extra time may seem like an eternity to you, but is just a blink of an eye to your client or customer. Frankly, I counsel myself (and other colleagues) to build in personal recovery time to ensure the path you are charging down at break-neck speed is the correct one, and not a one-way street to disaster.

It is vital that you view each day as a chance to make a new beginning! There will be days when your mood varies based on your new venture's progress. No matter what happened (good or bad) the previous day, you must remember that having your own business is a journey rather than a destination. In other words the learning, connections, and rewards, that make being an entrepreneur a richer life experience, happen all along the way

When I first thought of going out on my own a few years ago, a friend suggested I read *Success through a Positive Mental Attitude* by Napoleon Hill and W. Clement Stone. They said I would either be thrilled or terrified by the book and its message.

I found it a fantastic, quick read and source of true inspiration. The type of practical advice like DO IT NOW was a great help for someone like me, who has a natural tendency to procrastinate. The book lays out a simple, yet elegant approach to staying motivated and moving forward. I highly recommend this book as a resource that will enhance your ability to stay positive, an important first step to launch your entrepreneurial journey.

I hope that you now have a better sense of what qualities help to make a successful entrepreneur. Maintaining a blend of wisdom, flexibility risk-taking, innovation and commitment to action are critical traits. This is especially true in the rapidly growing and evolving Craft Beer industry.

There are a wide variety of ways for you to jumpstart your enterprise and build an enduring operation. No matter how you decide to enter this exciting business, whether running a brewpub, microbrewer, or contract brewery, you will yield a great return on your time and effort.

On so many levels craft brewing can be a fun, profitable, and engaging vocation. Selecting your brewery's name and brand identity, seeing throngs of people visit your new tasting room and having your beer featured at festivals are just a sample. Finding your latest tasty creations featured on end caps at big box stores and building recognition from your friends, colleagues and visitors ensure you create an experience that mirrors your own life and passion. No doubt, your deepest desires for success and acclaim will more than be satisfied as an entrepreneur. I encourage you to keep reading as I share with you how you and your team can build a profitable craft brewery!

Chapter Two

Buckle Up for an Amazing Journey!

So you are thinking seriously of becoming a craft brewer! You may have gotten the bug from a love of drinking beer, being a home brewer or visiting unique and different small breweries while travelling around the country. Jumping into this rapidly expanding business can be a total blast and a life-changing event at the same time. However, there is so much more to consider than just producing award-winning beers.

No matter how you have ignited this passion it helps to go back in time and understand how the craft brewing industry started. This is a fun trip down memory lane back to the early 1960's when the three big companies (Anheuser–Busch, Miller and Coors) primarily dominated the landscape. This chapter provides a time line in the evolution of this beverage segment along with key transformational events that make it a hot market today.

Plainly stated, craft beer is a beer that is not brewed by one of the big "mega-brewery" corporations. Generally, and more often than not, when the phrase craft beer is used, this is what it means. However, it is still inexact to define an industry or business by what it is *not*. so let's breakdown this description.

What is a Craft Beer?

It is critical for our conversation to understand exactly what is the cornerstone of this industry. The name craft beer or craft beer segment is worth investigating in greater detail. The Brewer's Association in Boulder, Colorado defines 'craft beer' as beer made by a brewer that is small, independent, and traditional. This description actually sums it up quite well and creates a common view so beer drinkers know what they are talking about. A more detailed breakdown would be as follows[1]:

- **Small** means brewing fewer than 6 million barrels of beer (approximately 3 percent of U.S. annual sales) per year, the federal limit for the small brewers excise tax exemption.

- **Independent** indicates that less than *25%* of the brewery is owned or controlled by a non-craft brewer.

- **Traditional** refers to a brewer that focuses on beers whose flavor derives from traditional or innovative brewing ingredients and their fermentation are made entirely or mostly from malt.

Yet, there is some excellent beer being made today by brewers that don't exactly fit these qualifications. So, it should be pointed out that just because beer *is* or *is not* considered 'craft beer,' this does not mean that the beer

---

[1] Revised Craft Brewer Definition - *Brewers Association*, (2014), Real Beer News, 20(3).

is good (or not). Meanwhile, in his history of craft beer, Tom Acitelli defines a craft brewery this way[2]:

> *This type of brewery includes any small, independently owned brewery that adheres to traditional brewing practices and ingredients. Craft brewers are distinct from larger regional and national breweries, which often use nontraditional ingredients and brew on a much vaster scale. (2013, p. xv)*

This definition incorporates two key elements that differentiate craft beer as unique: the **type of beer** and **size of the production facility** (although both metrics, "kind" and "size," tend be flexible notions among brew masters). By type of beer, craft beer describes different varieties of beer (e.g. ale, stout, porter, lager, etc.) yet typically not brewed with ingredients such as rice and corn.

Microbrew vs. Craft Beer

Can you remember back in the nineties when beer brewed by small, independent brewers was called microbrew? It seems kind of strange that the name disappeared. It was a great phase that perfectly described the new kind of breweries that were gaining market share back then. Everyone knew exactly what it meant and that

---

[2] The Audacity of Hops: The History of America's Craft Beer Revolution, Thomas Acitelli, Chicago Review Press, 2013

you as a beer expert would get an innovative and exciting beer if it came with the 'microbrew' name attached to it.

Meanwhile, numerous craft beer consumers (i.e. aficionados) associate the product with the overall small scale of the brewing facility: microbreweries and brewpubs. In general, microbreweries sell their output to a secondary source (i.e., a distributor or retailer); brewpubs are vertically integrated and sell directly to the consumer at the production point (i.e., its restaurant or bar). In addition, home brewing or Nano brewing is a further subset of small-scale production (usually limited to a capacity of three barrels or less)[3].

Nevertheless, The word microbrew fell mostly out of use for a couple of reasons. First, it is actually a legal term that precisely describes breweries of specific sizes in the US. To be considered a *microbrewery*, a brewery had to produce a limited number of barrels of beer, a *very* limited number. Second, the term just stopped making sense. Micro-breweries like Boston Beer Company (Sam Adams) and Sierra Nevada, grew to national distribution and gained plenty of brand recognition so they simply stopped being *micro*[4].

---

[3] A Brewer's Guide to Opening a Nano Brewery - Woodske, D.; *Self-published,* 2012
[4] Working Definition of Craft Beer - Eddings, B.; thespruce.com, 2017

The federal government looks at the craft industry in a totally different fashion: by the size of the production unit. Before 1978, the federal excise tax on beer was $9.00/barrel. In 1978, Congress reduced the levy on small brewers to $7.00/barrel for the first 60,000 barrels created by breweries with fewer than 2 million barrels in total annual sales. This created a significant windfall for these small craft producers with little thought that in less than 20 years an individual brewery (Boston Beer) would eclipse this cap[5].

Finally, "Big Beer", the beer produced by Anheuser-Busch/InBev (ABI) and MillerCoors, still account for the majority of malt beverages produced in the United States. In 2016 ABI and MillerCoors combined had a share of the market (SOM) of beer sales in the United States of 73% Comparatively, the craft beer segment comprises 12.3% of the domestic beer market (see Table 1)[6].

ABI and MillerCoors can be thought of as producing an ocean of beer while the craft beer segment produces only a small river. But that small river needs to

---

[5] Craft Beer in the United States: History, Numbers, and Geography - Kenneth G. Elzinga, Carol Horton Tremblay and Victor J. Tremblay; *Journal of Wine Economics*, Volume 10, Number 3, 2015, Pages 242–274

[6] Beer Industry Update – Annual, Beer Marketer's Insights

be put in perspective, because craft beer is still growing at better than 6% annually. Meanwhile, sales of beer with the Budweiser, Miller and Coors brands have been flat or declining in recent years.

ABI is the combination of the Belgian brewing firm InBev and Anheuser-Busch, which it acquired in 2008. MillerCoors is a joint venture between Coors and Miller, which took place in 2007. ABI's flagship brand in the United States is Budweiser (and the products and packages offered under that brand name). MillerCoors has two major brands: Miller and Coors (and the products and packages offered under those names). Now having this information as background we can take a look at how the craft brewing phenomenon was launched.

In the Beginning

Native Americans made a corn beer long before Europeans found their way to America. The Europeans brought with them their own version of beer. Although most of that was brewed in the home during the seventeenth and eighteenth centuries, a fledgling industry began to develop in 1612, when the first known New World brewery opened in New Amsterdam (now Manhattan).

The modern era of American beer began in the nineteenth century. In 1810 only 132 breweries operated and per capita consumption of commercially brewed beer amounted to less than a gallon. By 1873 the country had 4,131 breweries, a high water mark only surpassed again in 2016. In 1914, per capita consumption had grown to 20 gallons (compared to about 21.5 today). Then came National Prohibition[7].

American beer was already changing before Prohibition. When German immigrants began arriving in the middle of the nineteenth century they brought with them a thirst for all-malt lagers and the knowledge to brew them. But by the end of the century a) drinkers showed a preference for lighter-tasting lagers, ones that included corn or rice in the recipe, and b) consolidation began to eliminate many small, independently operated breweries. In 1918, the country had only one quarter the number of brewers that operated 45 years before.

National Prohibition began in January 1920 when the 18th Amendment, went into effect. It effectively ended in April 1933 with the return of 3.2% beer, and in December 1933 the 21st Amendment officially repealed the 18th. Within a year, 756 breweries were making beer, but the biggest companies remained intent on expansion, using production efficiencies and marketing to squeeze out smaller breweries.

---

[7] The American Beer Story – *Craftbeer.com/beer/beer-history*

The number of breweries shrunk quickly, to 407 in 1950 and 230 in 1961. By 1983 one source counted only 80 breweries, run by only 51 independent companies. Something else was happening as regional breweries closed. Not only were Northern Californians nurturing the rise of healthy cuisine and local wineries but also small breweries so new people didn't know what to call them.

The Godfather of Craft Beer

Fritz Maytag may be considered the true "father" of the modern craft brewing industry. He had been a consumer of Anchor Steam Beer when he heard the firm was going to go dark. The closure would mean the demise of the last brewery in the United States producing what would now be called craft beer.

Thus, Maytag purchased the assets of **Anchor Steam Beer Company** in 1965, although the firm had been in existence since 1896. Maytag's chief innovation was reinvigorating a fading company and a dying product. According to historical records, the firm had one employee at the time when Maytag began to learn the art and science of brewing in order to resurrect the firm and undertake the task of marketing the brand to bars and restaurants in the San Francisco Bay Area.

Although Maytag's pioneering endeavors took place in the United States, his influence on the market for beer has been global. Maytag and others who followed changed the conventional wisdom that the U.S. beer industry was destined to have a highly concentrated market structure, a homogeneous output (i.e., lager beer), and be insulated from the prospect of new entrants to the market.

There is a continuing discussion among historians that Anchor Brewing was not the first microbrewery because it saved an existing brewery rather than created an entirely new establishment. However, this perspective undervalues Maytag's contribution as by 1983 over 100 individuals had contacted him for advice and council about opening a microbrewery. This is an example of an entrepreneurial act repeated a thousand times over and across every state in the country.

The Early Brewers

Jack McAuliffe took beer-making skills that he had developed as a home brewer and combined them with his talent for welding, his training as an engineer, and his experience as an electrician to form **New Albion Brewing Company** in 1976. Stimulating McAuliffe's transition from home brewing to small-scale commercial production was a visit to Maytag's operation.

Having settled in Sonoma, California, McAuliffe was one of the first to recognize the demand for craft beer as a drink to be paired with food. Up until this point in time it was the business model of the wine industry. He also demonstrated that small-scale production could develop a product whose taste signature stimulated the demand for craft beer. In doing so, McAuliffe influenced other craft brewers. Unfortunately, New Albion exited the market in 1982 primarily because it was too small to be profitable.

As a high school student, **Ken Grossman** read a book by Fred Eckhardt, *A Treatise on Lager Beers (1983)*, and began home brewing. A few years later, he was teaching home brewing in Colorado. At this time, he visited the brewing facilities of McAuliffe and Maytag and left with both inspiration and information. Gifted with the same mechanical skills as McAuliffe, Grossman originally partnered with Paul Camusi to found the Sierra Nevada Brewing Company in Chico, California, which opened its doors in 1981. In 2014, the **Sierra Nevada Company** opened a brewery far from the Sierra Nevada mountains: a 350,000 barrel facility near Asheville, North Carolina. In 2013, the Sierra Nevada firm was the second-largest craft brewer, with sales of almost 1 million barrels.

Jim Koch was born into a family with a brewing history but began his career at the Boston Consulting Group, where his clients were anything but craft brewers. His family urged him not to consider brewing as a livelihood—advice that he took for a while and then rejected.

Unlike McAuliffe and Grossman, Koch lacked skills in cobbling together pipes and kettles, but he had management expertise and experience when he founded the **Boston Beer Company**. Rather than build a craft brewery from scratch, Koch adopted the business model of using the facilities of an incumbent brewer (Pittsburgh Brewing Company) to produce craft beer to his specifications. He essentially bought capacity at marginal cost. The irony that Koch's brand, Samuel Adams, was being brewed at a facility accustomed to turning out the Iron City brand was not lost on some purists in the craft beer movement.

Eventually, the Boston Beer Company integrated vertically into brewing, but this was after the Samuel Adams brand portfolio had become the best-selling craft beer in the United States. The Boston Brewing Company's output of almost 2.3 million barrels in 2013 handily exceeded the cap for the tax exemption designed to aid the craft beer segment, allowing Koch to join the Bloomberg Billionaires Index the following year.

The Early Promoters

Three individuals brought the message of craft beer to a much broader audience by stimulating the demand for this growing segment. The three who merit mention are Fred Eckhardt, Charles Papazian, and Michael Jackson.

The increase in demand for craft brewing was achieved through the sharing of information about (1) home brewing, which weaned many beer consumers away from the lager products of Big Beer; (2) craft beer production; and (3) beer as a beverage that can be easily paired with food, rather than as a liquid that quenched thirst on a hot day or offered an inexpensive buzz.

Home brewing remains such an important introduction to the purchase of commercially produced craft beer that the Brewers Association (the trade association for craft brewers) promotes **the** American Homebrewers Association (AHA).

After a visit to Maytag's brewery, Fred Eckhardt began to brew craft beer at home that was designed to mimic the quality of Anchor Steam. In addition to home brewing for his own consumption, Eckhardt taught home brewing to others and out of this came his book, *A Treatise on Lager Beers*, published in 1970 (which influenced Ken Grossman). Thousands of copies of this book were sold; the widespread practice of home brewing led in turn to the reversal of many state laws (rarely enforced) that banned home brewing.

It appears there is no other U.S. industry in which home production led to more commercial start-ups than took place in craft beer. Those who engaged in home brewing changed their beer preferences; they became more likely to select brands of craft beer when consuming at the local tavern. Home brewing acquainted many consumers with the flavors and qualities of different kinds of beer. It also led pioneers like Jim McAuliffe and Ken Grossman to begin their own commercial ventures.

Charles Papazian was not a producer of craft beer but rather a promoter of the product that others were commercially producing. He founded the AHA and also wrote about home brewing in *The Complete Joy of Homebrewing (1984)*. Those individuals who joined his crusade developed tastes for beers that made them customers of the craft beer segment. It also made them apostles of craft beer to their friends; those who did not home brew became customers of those who brewed commercially.

Papazian's organization of the Great American Beer Festival (GABF), first held in 1982 in Boulder, was a harbinger of craft beer promotion. People came to sample beer and paid to do so. The beer festival was an eye opener for city officials because social events centered on craft beer did not turn into drunken brawls or occasions for municipal property damage.

The Great American Beer Festival and its progeny were not like college spring breaks at beachside cities. Beer festivals brought people from out of town with discretionary income to be spent not only on craft beer but also restaurants and lodging. Today, no city would turn down an application for a beer festival. Indeed, a small industry has sprung up to organize and promote these festivals.

Finally, the writer Michael Jackson became to beer what Robert Parker Jr. was to wine. Jackson's book, *The World Guide to Beer (1988)*, was the first to reach a broad audience about the tastes of different beers. Jackson did give favorable mention to Maytag's Anchor Steam Beer company. Jackson's writings acquainted millions of readers with what he called the "beer style"—beers from Asia, Europe, and the Caribbean were discussed and explained. At the time that American readers were coming to understand beer other than Big Beer, the craft segment was starting to ramp up in order to provide a superior product.

The craft beer segment in the United States would not be what it is without Jackson's influence as an informant about the vast multiplicity of beers that were being brewed and, starting with Fritz Maytag, came to be brewed in the United States to satisfy curious or intrepid consumers.

Chapter Three

Getting "Hopped Up" on Craft Beer!

Congratulations! **You have made up your mind to jump "head first" into owning your own brewery.** So how did you get to this point? We can start by assuming you have some experience making your own "home brewed" craft beer.

I suspect that you began in your kitchen weaving together small quantities of various malts and hops into unique and distinctive beverages. The enticing aroma wafting from your range put a "hop" in your step! This desire to experiment consistently grew until now, that you have a 3-barrel Nano system in your home or garage.

Meanwhile, a variety of friends and family have been enjoying your home brew success over the past few years. The positive feedback received led you to drop off samples at bars and restaurants in the 10-mile area immediately around your home. Now, you are getting orders for logs (1/6 barrels) to be put on tap at 25 to 30 locations.

Wow, it is truly a blast seeing your beer being sucked down at local taverns and now you are making more than some spending change in the process. Now that you are hopped up on craft brewing you gather a few good buddies together and start discussing what it would take to jump into this fast growing business full-time.

This leads to a whole list of key questions that need to be answered for instance... How much space will I need for my brewery and what type of equipment should I purchase? What style of beer should I make and how much volume should I expect to sell my first few years in the business? How will I get my product into stores and restaurants for sale?

Before taking on those thorny questions we should take a few minutes and examine how to actually brew your beer. Following is a simple breakdown of the process for you, your friends and colleagues to review, as they join you in the craft brewery business.

This review is a critical starting point before you tackle more technical aspects of your business. Since your team has probably spent more time drinking your IPA's I thought a refresher would be helpful for all interested parties!

What is the process of brewing beer?

Let's face it, learning all there is to know about brewing would take many years of study. There are so many nuances between making a lackluster lager and producing a gold medal winning Scottish Ale. In addition, you would probably have to get one or more advanced degrees, before becoming a legendary brewmaster.

Luckily, all of that technical background isn't needed to enjoy beer. A cursory understanding of what happens in the brewhouse is useful for beer connoisseurs to have, since almost all of the flavors encountered when tasting beer were the result of what happened while it was being brewed.

Beer is made from four basic ingredients: barley, water, hops and yeast. Before you get rolling, you must decide what style of beer you want to make. That decision, whether to do a hop forward IPA, creamy oatmeal stout or double red ale, impacts a whole range of choices. Below is a picture diagramming the overall brewing process[1].

---

[1] Infographic of Brewing Process – *CanStock Photo*

You will remember, craft beer is a combination of the fab four of choice ingredients blended using a tested recipe to make a memorable brew. It is so much more than any one element individually when placed in the hands of a skilled brewer. You will need to consider the impact of each of the following elements as you make great beers for all that visit your brewery. Here is a brief summary of the key components.

Ingredients

barley   hops   water   yeast

Malted Barley – This ingredient is the core source of the unique color, flavor, and body in a finished beer. Before this can become the "heart and soul" used for brewing, barley must first be malted, where it is immersed in water to induce germination. The sprouted barley is then rapidly kiln dried.

Malted barley can be roasted to varying degrees to influence beer flavor and color. This range includes pale malts (delicate bread-like flavors), lightly caramelized malts (subtle toffee notes and amber coloring) and deeply roasted malts (chocolate or coffee characteristic and coloring) and many other choices in between. Many brew masters look to pre-made commercially available malts for time, cost and storage considerations.

Hops – This component provides the aroma, bitterness, spice and preservative characteristics to your brew. Today, your brew masters can source dozens of hop flower types with unique aromas that range from floral to citrus to earth to pine. Hops when added at the start of the boil contribute primarily to the bitter flavor of beer, while hops added at the conclusion of the boil contribute aroma to a beer.

Water – This is the most prevailing ingredient in all types of beer and it plays a significant and often overlooked role in the making of a great brew. Clearly, great tasting water can produce amazing beer. Nevertheless your astute brewer must carefully assess the pH and mineral content of their water source. This is why some breweries will use a reverse osmosis system to give the water the exact character desired to match the style of beer being created.

Yeast – While this ingredient is not visible to the naked eye it ultimately unleashes the "magic" that makes a great brew. Your brewers use these microscopic yeast cells to convert fermentable sugars into alcohol and carbon dioxide, thereby creating craft beer. Yeast is often thought of as the soul of a beer, as it dramatically shapes the finished product. In fact, various types of ale yeast strains are noted for providing fruity esters and spicy phenols to beer, while wild yeast strains provide a tart quality.

Ultimately, your brew master must consider the quantities of ingredients needed, whether to include specialty items, ideal temperature and duration of brewing time and any additional processes critical to making a specific style of beer[2].

---

[2] Brewing Process - *Craft Brewers Guild; craftbrewersguildma.com*

1. Malting

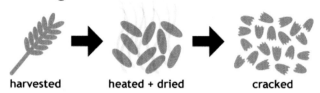

harvested   heated + dried   cracked

The brewing process starts with grains, usually barley (although sometimes wheat, rye or other such things.) The grains are harvested and processed through a process of heating, drying out and cracking.

A mill cracks open the malted barley kernels with steel rollers, exposing the starches inside. Starches convert to sugar and later convert to alcohol. These broken kernels are referred to as "grist." The main goal of malting is to isolate the enzymes needed for brewing so that it's ready for the next step.

2. Mashing

Next, the grist goes into the mash tun, where hot water is added to make "mash" with a porridge-like consistency. In just about an hour, the hot water has acted as a catalyst to convert starches in the grains into sugars.

The result is called the "wort", a mixture of barley husks and sweet liquid.

Once the desired wort is arrived upon, the temperature is jacked up to 170 degrees, ending the chemical process completely. The result is a wort that is less viscous and easier to separate from the mash. This is what's known as mashing out.

3. Boiling

The wort is collected from the lauter tun and is transferred to the brew kettle. Your brewer checks to make sure that the sugar concentration is at the desired level. It's measured as a sugar percentage by weight, and is known as the original gravity of the wort. The wort is boiled, and then hops are added.

The boiling does three things: first, it sterilizes the wort so that later, when yeast is added, the yeast is the only microorganism in the wort. Second, it extracts the bitterness from the hops, flavoring the beer to the brewer's design. Lastly, it coagulates malt proteins so that they can be skimmed out along with the hops.

After the first round of hops, additional hops can be added. The hops added later are typically for aroma, as these hops are not in the kettle long enough for the aromatics to be boiled away. The brew kettle step typically takes no more than two hours. After that duration, the wort could become more bitter than desired.

4. Fermentation

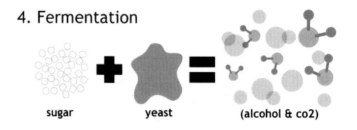

sugar   yeast   (alcohol & co2)

Once the hour-long boil is over the wort is cooled, strained and filtered. It's then put in a fermenting vessel and yeast is added to it. At this point the brewing is complete and the fermentation begins. The fermentation tanks mark the only time oxygen is freely introduced and in contact with the liquid

The beer is stored for a couple of weeks at room temperature (in the case of ales) or many weeks at cold temperatures (in the case of lagers) while the yeast works its fermentation magic. Basically the yeast eats up all that sugar in the wort and spits out CO_2 and alcohol as waste products.

The reaction of the yeast causes the temperature of the liquid to rise and brewers watch this closely, taking cooling measures as needed. The liquid needs to stay at an acceptable temperature range for the specific beer being brewed. The wort can now be called beer!

5. Bottling & Aging

You've now got alcoholic beer, however it is still flat and uncarbonated. The flat beer is bottled, at which time it is either artificially carbonated like a soda, or if it's going to be 'bottle conditioned' it's allowed to naturally carbonate via the CO_2 the yeast produces. After allowing it to age for anywhere from a few weeks to a few months you drink the beer, and it's delicious!

So that is a quick reminder of how your brew master makes a unique and tasty beer in small batches. There are now over 150 different styles that can be made by varying the types of ingredients, quantities, temperatures and fermentation times.

Chapter Four

Size Really Does Matter!

A question I often encounter from new teams is what is the optimal size I should build my new brewery? I decided the best way to answer this inquiry and share critical information is through reaching out to an experienced industry insider. Let me tell you about an individual who has lived beer all his life. I recently connected with **Jeff Browning** who is a partner and Brewmaster at a new concept brewpub/restaurant in Bridgeport (CT).

Brewport Brewing Company is focused on creating a family friendly atmosphere where they offer simple fare such as thin crust pizza from wood fired ovens and unique salads. The team offers 8 to 10 craft beers specifically developed on-site and up to 20 guest taps so visitors get the best of both worlds.

Jeff started collecting beer cans in the early 70's and has amassed a large collection of memorabilia (~40,000 items) from Connecticut brewers including their historic recipes. He began brewing beer in his bedroom closet at home when he was just a teenager (without his parents ever finding out) just because it was "cool". Throughout high school he was making his own mead and cider for consumption with friends and learning more about home brewing along the way. This led him to researching all he could about the origin and critical elements for making different types of beer.

Jeff ultimately had the chance to convert his passion into a career. He took over both marketing and brewing for several early entries into the modern craft beer business (in the early 90's).

Jeff has an intriguing perspective on the current industry growth trends and what makes a brewery successful. **First, it is imperative that you really have a great product.** He said "Just because your mama (or a buddy) tells you your beer tastes great does not actually make it so". While this seems like such a straightforward concept you still see novice brewers today that are making either really great and memorable ales, stouts and lagers or truly terrible beers. It is vital to receive real outside validation before jumping head- long into the business and buying a load of very expensive equipment.

Second, Jeff indicated that the most expensive components in brewing beer today are time and labor. It is expensive to bring in professional brewers to augment your team and help differentiate your product. In fact, it takes the same amount to time to produce 3 BBL or 30 BBL depending on the equipment you are using. Thus, utilizing a larger scale brewhouse will help drive down the cost per ounce to produce your beer and help maintain improved quality as well.

How Does This Impact Craft Brewing?

I would like to further breakdown this concept of efficiency and how it applies to the burgeoning craft brewing industry. In fact, producing craft beer involves the economist's traditional triad of land, labor, and capital.

- "Land" constitutes such inputs as the grain and hops that go into the brewing process.

- Human input or "labor", in addition to the entrepreneur who starts the firm, consists of employees who oversee how the beer is brewed, packaged and then put into distribution.

- Meanwhile, "capital" equipment consists of storage facilities for natural ingredients, the brew kettles and fermenters needed for the brewing process, and the packaging equipment (for kegs, bottles, and, increasingly, cans).

During the early days of craft brewing (e.g. the 1970s), a barrier to new firms entering the business was the absence of a market for purchasing capital assets. Ultimately, start-ups had to build or cobble together equipment to brew in small batches. Meanwhile, equipment manufacturers typically were set up to meet the demand of Big Beer with line speeds of over 1,000 bottles or cans per minute.

Clearly, this size and speed were over kill for your average craft brewer. So the industry's pioneers regularly sourced machinery and equipment from other industries and adapted it to brewing and packaging malt beverages.

Early entrants often swapped ideas about how to gather the necessary capital equipment to brew and package their output. All this has changed dramatically in our current marketplace. A craft brewer today can easily purchase turnkey canning equipment that runs from 50 to 250 cans per minute meeting their specific needs.

Numerous vendors for malt, brewhouse technology, labeling equipment, and other services means that it is no longer necessary for you as a new entrant to have skills as a welder, plumber, and electrician to be a craft brewer or, absent these skills, find a large brewer with excess capacity.

How Do Craft Breweries Breakdown by Size?

An important element for your team to consider is how does the craft brewing industry assess size. In general, this is based upon the number of barrel equivalents that a brewery sells annually.

Let's start by looking at the overall industry breakdown. At year-end 2016, there were 5,234 craft brewers in operation with only 186 (or less than 4%) considered to be regional brewers with production in excess of 15,000 barrels annually. The following chart details the historical trend in the United States.

U.S. Craft Brewery Count by Category

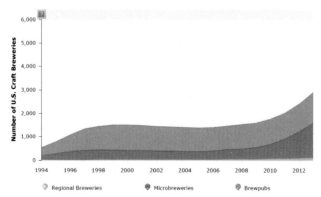

In fact, recent statistics put together by the Brewery Association show some startling trends. First, you are part of an extremely fragmented industry where 92% of the companies produce fewer than 7,500 barrels annually[1].

U.S. Brewery Count

	2012	2013	2014	2015	2016	'15 to '16 % Change
CRAFT	2,420	2,898	3,734	4,504	5,234	+ 16.2
Regional Craft Breweries	97	119	135	178	186	+ 4.5
Microbreweries	1,143	1,471	2,071	2,596	3,132	+ 20.6
Brewpubs	1,180	1,308	1,528	1,730	1,916	+ 10.8
LARGE NON-CRAFT	23	23	26	30	51	
OTHER NON-CRAFT	32	31	20	14	16	
Total U.S. Breweries	2,475	2,952	3,780	4,548	5,301	+ 16.6

---

[1] Number of Breweries - *Brewers Association;*
brewersassociation.com

Your new brewery, over time, should reach a sales level that places it as a large microbrewer (between 7,500 and 14,999 bbls) in order to ensure sustainable profitability and a base to grow. This is a major hurdle to growing a business that can eventually be sold to a larger entity such as an In Bev or Miller Coors.

How Do You Figure Out Capacity?.

So how do you actually get started? A key question that immediately comes to mind is how many barrels of beer will be produced annually in your new craft brewery. This is a critical piece of data that will impact all the planning that you and your team do going forward for several key reasons.

First, it affects how much space you will need for the actual brewhouse (i.e. brew kettles, fermenters and packaging equipment). Second, the annual production calculation also has an impact of how much storage will be needed for raw materials, dry goods, refrigerated components and finished product. Third, the brewhouse size will also impact the amount and complexity of additional equipment (e.g. forklifts, cooperage, pallets) that will need to be kept in-house to handle market demand for your exquisite beer.

Now with that background lets dive further into assessing the equipment size required for your projected brewing frequency and total volume of desired annual production. Remember, the sizing and selection of a system is critical to the operational efficiency and overall profitability of a brewery.

You can use this information as a basic guideline to system configuration[2].

Calculation of Annual Production

Annual Production = System Size (Brewhouse Size) x Number of brews per week x 50 weeks per year

Example: 10 Barrel system x 3 brews/week x 50 weeks/year = 1,500 barrels (bbls)/year

Projection of Fermenters Required

Desired Annual Production = Number of Fermenters (to meet desired annual production)

(Brewhouse Size x Vessel Cycles/year)

Sizing for a Brewpub – Example

Parameters

"1000 barrels per year; 75% Ales, 25% Lagers"

50 brewing weeks/year

14 Day Ales / 28 Day Lagers with full fermentation in fermenters

Ales – 25 cycles/fermenter/year (50 brewing weeks/2 week fermentation)

Lagers – 12.5 cycles / fermenter / year (50 brewing weeks/4 week fermentation)

6 beers on tap

Calculate system size and number of fermenters

---

[2] Brewery System Sizing Overview – *Specific Mechanical Systems Ltd.*; specificmechanical.com

For example:

3.5 barrel system 1000 barrels / year / 3.5 barrel system / 50 brewing weeks/year = 5.8 brews per week

7 barrel system 1000 barrels / year / 7 barrel system / 50 brewing weeks/year = 2.9 brews per week

10 barrel system 1000 barrels / year / 10 barrel system / 50 brewing weeks/year = 2 brews per week

15 barrel system 1000 barrels / year / 15 barrel system / 50 brewing weeks/year = 1.3 brews per week

Comment – One must look at the labor component in selecting a system size.

Most properly sized brewpubs brew 2 – 3 times per week in their first couple of years of operation.

"Brewing less than twice a week, the system may have been oversized to start with."

"Brewing more than 3 times a week, the system may have been initially undersized."

"For this example, either the 7 or 10 barrel system is recommended."

Number of fermenters required

Projected: 750 bbls Ales (75%) & 250 bbls Lagers (25%)

For 7 barrel system

Ales ——> 750 bbls / year / (7 bbls x 25 cycles/year) = 4.2 = 5 Fermenters

Lagers ——> 250 bbls / year / (7 bbls x 12.5 cycles/year) = 2.8 = 3 Fermenters

Total ——> 7 – 8 Fermenters to produce 750 bbls Ales and 250 bbls Lagers

For 10 barrel system

Ales ——> 750 bbls / year / (10 bbls x 25 cycles/year) = 3 Fermenters

Lagers ——> 250 bbls / year / (10 bbls x 12.5 cycles/year) = 2 Fermenters

Total ——> 5 Fermenters to produce 750 bbls Ales and 250 bbls Lagers

Number of Serving Vessels ; Equals number of desired beer styles one wishes to serve via tank to tap.

Note number of beer styles may increase through kegging and/or bottling.

System Recommendation: 10 barrel system with 5 x 10 barrel fermenters and 6 x 10 barrel serving tanks.

Selecting the 10 barrel system over the 7 barrel system has the following benefits:

- Good utilization of manpower (2 brews per week)
- Reduced floor space (5 fermenters vs. 8 fermenter)
- Better priced/more economical (fewer fermenters)
- Better expansion capabilities
- Meets all system requirements

Note: *Double sized fermenters (and conditioning tanks) may half the number of vessels required to meet annual production. All calculations assume 50 brewing weeks per year*

What is a Target Efficiency Level?

The charts below provide some general ranges on the sizing of brew house systems for both brew pubs and microbreweries. A benchmark that you may want to consider is the following. **Your aim is to have your brewery operating at approximately 85% of its overall capacity.** When you fall below that level your production methods are inefficient, resulting in a higher cost per barrel brewed. Conversely, when your facility reaches the 90% level or above then you run the risk of not being able to meet the marketplace demand for your beers because you are tapped out of space.

You will experience a constant juggling act between deciding when to add additional capital equipment for your anticipated new level of production and saving that money for other pressing needs such as marketing. A strategy that many successful breweries have employed is acquiring a large enough initial brewhouse system (e.g. 15 bbl vs 10 bbl).to get up and rolling. Then the overall capacity can be expanded in the interim with the addition of more fermenters for aging the product.

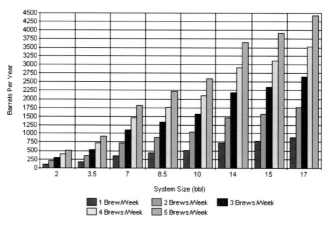

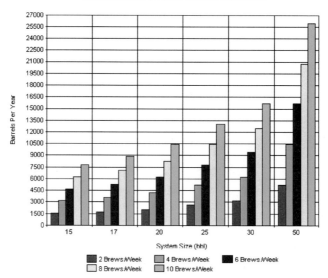

In order to read this chart pick the size of brewery you are looking for then choose how many brews per week you wish to produce and correspond that with the barrels per year on the left hand side of the chart.

	Number of Brews / Week								
	1			2			3		
System Size (Barrels)	Annual (Barrels)	Weekly Average (Pints)	Beer Sales (Weekly) @ $3.00 / Pint	Annual (Barrels)	Weekly Average (Pints)	Beer Sales (Weekly) @ $3.00 / Pint	Annual (Barrels)	Weekly Average (Pints)	Beer Sales (Weekly) @ $3.00 / Pint
2	100	477	1431	200	954	2862	300	1431	4293
3.5	175	835	2504	350	1670	5009	525	2504	7513
5	250	1193	3578	500	2385	7155	750	3578	10733
7	350	1670	5009	700	3339	10017	1050	5009	15026
8.5	425	2027	6082	850	4055	12164	1275	6082	18245
10	500	2385	7155	1000	4770	14310	1500	7155	21465
14	700	3339	10017	1400	6678	20034	2100	10017	30051
15	750	3578	10733	1500	7155	21465	2250	10733	32198
17	850	4055	12164	1700	8109	24327	2550	12164	36491

There is so much to absorb in how you effectively size your facility to maximize the value of the investment capital you have available. In addition, you want to ensure that the equipment purchased can be easily upgraded to meet expanded sales.

You should now have a much better idea of how large a brewery you need to get rolling with your dream! This chapter also offers some additional guidance for those brewers looking to jump from microbrewery to regional players. The next chapter will change our focus to the marketing and branding side of building a profitable craft brewing business.

Chapter Five

How Much Do You Know About Al Capone?

This chapter is intended to provide some historical background on how beer is regulated around the country and prohibition's impact on today's marketplace. I will begin with some simple details of how the government has taxed beer over the past 50+ years.

National Prohibition began January 16, 1920 when the 18th Amendment, also known as the Volstead Act, went into effect. The impact was a declared national ban on the manufacture, sale, transportation, importation, and exportation of intoxicating liquors for beverage purposes. It effectively ended in April 1933 with the return of 3.2% beer, and in December 1933 the 21st Amendment officially repealed the 18th.

From the enactment of the Volstead Act, prohibition agents hunted down bootleggers, who were growing enormously powerful and rich by smuggling liquor into the United States primarily from Canada and Europe.

Criminal syndicates completely controlled the liquor industry. Assassinations, bombs, bullets and corruption were routine; every industry paid tribute, directly or indirectly, to bootleggers and gangsters who had forged such close ties with local authorities that anonymous prohibition enforcement squads became necessary in some cities. Chicago was one of those cities

Al Capone, was one of the most famous American gangsters, also known as "Scarface," who rose to infamy as the leader of the Chicago mafia during the Prohibition era.

By some estimates, his crime syndicate pulled in around $100 million a year, the largest portion from bootlegging, followed by gambling, prostitution, racketeering and other illicit activities.

Capone was dubbed "Public Enemy No. 1" after arranging the infamous St. Valentine's Day Massacre of major gang rivals in 1929. Ultimately, he was sent to Alcatraz Prison in 1934 for a tax evasion conviction.[1]

Chicago belonged entirely to Al Capone. The collective force of 3,000 police officers and 300 prohibition agents failed to bring down Capone's empire. The lack of prohibition convictions in a city as wet as Chicago only cemented the fact that Capone was buying protection from law enforcement.

Do You Remember the Untouchables?

Do you remember the movie "The Untouchables" from 1987 starring Kevin Costner and Sean Connery? It

---

[1] Al Capone – Biography; biography.com

told the story of Special Agent Eliot Ness who was one of the most famous federal agents in the history of law enforcement. Ness supervised an ordinary team of agents and against all odds; he and his Untouchables did the extraordinary by breaking the back of organized crime in Chicago in the 1930's. He performed brilliantly as both a crime fighter and a leader in a time of national distress.

When Ness and his Untouchables emerged as the enforcers who finally put away Al Capone, they became so ingrained in the American psyche that cartoonist, Chester Gould, launched a new comic strip based on the crime stories publicized in the daily headlines[3].

---

[3] SA Eliot Ness, a Legacy ATF Agent – Bureau of Alcohol, Tobacco, Firearms and Explosives (ATF); atf.gov

Using Eliot Ness as his model, Dick Tracy was born. For decades thereafter, Eliot Ness and his fictional alter ego would influence American notions of detective work, crime fighting and heroism.

The real Eliot Ness' success was no accident. During his 10 years of Federal law enforcement service with various ATF's legacy agencies, he faced organized criminal elements who were flush with huge sums of cash from these various illegal ventures. All the while, he demonstrated that he possessed intelligence, ability and above all else, honesty and integrity, which he undisputedly maintained throughout his Federal, law enforcement career.

His team of agents, later given the moniker "the Untouchables", not only wreaked havoc on gangster Al Capone's criminal empire, but also went on to successfully apprehend many of Chicago's notorious gangsters and bootleggers.

Perhaps what is most remarkable about Ness is not that he and his squad sent Capone packing for the penitentiary; but that he (Ness) later went on to lead two additional teams of agents in the cleanup of two equally crime-ridden cities protected by corrupt law enforcement agencies Cincinnati and Cleveland.

A Brief History of Alcohol Regulation

The Bureau of Alcohol, Tobacco, Firearms and Explosives (BATFE) is a federal law enforcement and regulatory agency with a substantial history dating back to the tax-collecting bureaucracy of the 1800s.

This oldest tax-collecting Treasury agency traces its roots back to when Congress imposed a tax on imported spirits to help pay the Revolutionary War debt in 1789. In 1862, Congress created an Office of Internal Revenue, also within the Treasury Department.

The new commissioner was charged with collection of taxes on alcohol and tobacco. In 1863, Congress authorized enforcement measures within the office to aid in collecting and offsetting criminal evasion, and soon after added legal counsel for prosecution—both features that continue under today's ATF.

Until recently, nearly all federal regulations involving alcohol were issued by the Treasury Department Bureau of Alcohol, Tobacco, and Firearms (BATF), established by the Federal Alcohol Administration Act of 1935 and the 1968 Gun Control Act.

However, in 2002, under the Homeland Security Act, the Bureau was divided. The part remaining in the Department of the Treasury was renamed the Alcohol and Tobacco Tax and Trade Bureau (TTB). A new Bureau of Alcohol, Tobacco, Firearms and Explosives (ATF) was formed in the Department of Justice. **The TTB is responsible for administering and regulating the operations of distilleries, wineries, and breweries, as well as importers and wholesalers in the industry.**

A selection of key functions that TTB has primary responsible related to beer brewing include:

- **Brewery Application Approval** – In order to qualify as a brewery you must complete and submit to the TTB all appropriate forms along with any other required supporting documentation. The TTB will typically complete its screening process within sixty days after receiving a completed Brewers Notice packet.

- **Excise Tax Collection** - U.S. Government involvement in the beer industry also includes taxation. The current federal excise tax on beer, in effect since January 1, 1991, is $18 per barrel for

31 gallons. However, a reduced tax rate applies, at a rate of $7 per barrel, to the first 60,000 barrels of beer removed for consumption or sale by brewing companies that do not produce more than 2,000,000 barrels of beer per calendar year. The federal excise tax regulations also include other rules, including for removals without tax payment and inter-brewery purchases.

- **Labeling and Advertising Approval** - The TTB implements and enforces a broad range of statutory and compliance provisions to ensure that alcohol products are created, labeled, and advertised in accordance with Federal laws and regulations. Brewers must follow the labeling and advertising requirements found at 27 CFR Part 7, *Labeling and Advertising of Malt Beverages* and 27 CFR Part 16, *Alcoholic Beverage Health Warning Statement*.

- **Home Brewing** - Any adult may produce beer, without payment of tax, for personal or family use and not for sale. An adult is any individual who is 18 years of age or older. If the locality in which the household is located requires a greater minimum age for the sale of beer to individuals, the adult shall be that age before commencing the production of beer. This exemption does not authorize the production of beer for use contrary to state or local law.[4]

---

[4]Government Beer Regulations – Apex Publishers; *beer-brewing.com*, Chapter 22

Where Do You Sell Your Craft Brews?

Now with some history about Eliot Ness, prohibition, bootlegging and regulation by the federal government; let's get into where and how you can sell your craft brews. We will start by reviewing the two main types of retail outlets that will likely sell your delicious product.

The information provided will touch on the options available for your team to distribute these unique new craft beers. There are various different locations where connoisseurs will gather for the latest IPA, Amber Ale or Gose. It is critical to understand those sales locations and how you actually get space on the store shelves or taps.

First, there are On-Premise **accounts** represented by restaurants, bars and brewpubs. These establishments typical sell beer by the glass from an elaborate tap system or by the individual bottle. Many offer a wide selection of craft beers, ciders and other handcrafted spirits. In fact, increasingly even brewpubs will carry other well-known regional brands as "guest beers". This gives the craft beer enthusiast a chance to sample other products not normally found in your home marketplace.

The goal of your brewery is to secure as many "lines" as possible at a single outlet. Typically, greater on-site availability directly translates into increased sales activity. The sales your team makes to these locations will be in the form of either Half Barrels or Logs (1/6 barrel).

71

The second type of retail channel is **Off-Premise accounts**. This category includes package stores, grocery stores, wholesale clubs, warehouse outlets and other similar establishments. The owners sell craft beer in bottles and cans as both six-pack and 12 pack combinations. In addition, the product is available both chilled from coolers and warm in displays on the sales floor.

The focus for your team is getting multiple placements of products including end aisle stacks using point of purchase merchandising. This is considered the location where the consumer has a full choice of which malt beverage to buy.

The more you can connect your brand to the craft beer lover, the higher your sales will be. This is also the channel where product sampling can make a tremendous difference in stimulating impulse buying. Clearly, once the connoisseur tastes your beer they will want to come back for more!

Specialty and seasonal beer sales from small and independent craft brewers are arguably the most diverse and exciting group of brands that beer distributors bring to market. This powerhouse group of beers makes a major impact in the chain and convenience channels. Nearly 20 percent of sales from craft brewers are made up of seasonal beers. In the five months between July and November, nearly 60 percent of all seasonal beers are typically sold. There is nothing like this category in any other alcohol segment. In 2015, the total sales in this segment, which is only a small window into craft, almost eclipsed $17 million dollars![5]

How Does Your Beer Get Delivered to the Marketplace?

So now you have signed up a variety of restaurants, bars, liquor stores and brew pubs to handle your expanding craft brand portfolio. The next key question for your team is how your amazing beer gets to the marketplace. There are two primary approaches that are being used by craft brewers today.

A brewery can self distribute using a **two-tier** distribution system. This is the approach where your team sells to the retail outlet without a "middleman". It involves having your own vehicles to bring kegs, logs, bottles and cans directly to the consumer outlet.

The primary benefit is that you as the brewery make a significantly higher profit margin on each unit sold and maintain control of your local market distribution. In addition, it provides your team the opportunity to deliver an elevated service level. The distributor takes a major cut for facilitating the movement of beer from the brewer to

---

[5] Seasonal Beer Management Best Practices for Distributors – *Brewers Association; brewersassociation.com*

the retailer. Therefore, your enterprise can work efficiently while servicing customers within a 20 miles radius without requiring outside distribution help. Clearly, distributors make their money by selling large volumes with small margins.

This option also presents a number of key challenges. First, the amount of area that can be effectively covered when your sales rapidly expand is very limited. The in-house manpower required to load vehicles, deliver product and collect cooperage (e.g. empty logs and kegs) can quickly overwhelm the enhanced sales. In general, this option works best for the home brewer that is initially expanding his network to a group of 25 to 30 accounts.

Eventually, at around the 3,000 annual barrel sales level, your craft brewery will reach a critical mass. At this point, you will need to establish relationships with traditional distributors.

The advent of the third party distribution system or three-tier network harkens back to the Prohibition Era in the US. This was the time when a nationwide constitutional ban on the production, importation, transportation and sale of alcoholic beverages was passed by Congress and remained in place from 1920 to 1933.

The original premise, which eventually resulted in the thinking put forward by activists in the 19th century, was to cure various societal ills (e.g. alcoholism, family violence, and saloon based political corruption) by ending the alcoholic beverage trade[6].

When Prohibition was repealed through the enactment of the 21st Amendment, a new distribution system was subsequently put into place where brewers could only sell to retailers through a distributor. This system was set up to eliminate practices where beer producers, directly or indirectly, coerced retailers that were partially owned by them to favor brands from certain producers (i.e. themselves). The insulator of choice was the distributor.

Today, you will find independent beer distributors, licensed by both the federal and state governments; these enterprises facilitate the delivery of bottles, cans, cases and kegs from a brewer to the shelf of your favorite local restaurant, tavern or liquor store. In addition, these entities work to help new brands get to market and ensure that consumers can choose from a vast selection of beer.

Brewers & Importers   Distributors   Retailers

---

[6] Prohibition in the United States – *Wikipedia; Wikipedia.com*

Beer distributors source beer from a wide variety of importers and manufacturers. By working with numerous brewers, distributors provide a vehicle to market for the largest multinational beer brands to start-up craft brewers. Because of this system, you can order a California craft beer off a menu in Illinois; enjoy a Connecticut brew in a Tennessee restaurant; and see a tap handle from Pennsylvania in a Texas bar.

This <u>three-tier system</u> provides the infrastructure; capital and personnel small brewers need to reach a wide network of retailers. Distributors' infrastructure includes state-of-the-art warehouses and fleets of temperature-controlled trucks and vehicles that preserve these perishable products. Distributor personnel include not only employees that handle warehousing, transporting and delivering all types of beer to local retailers, but also sales and merchandising professionals who help promote each label of beer they sell. Distributors deliver customized inventory based on the requirements of each individual retailer in their local market[7].

The craft beer industry is limited geographically because of industry structure and segmentation. In terms of structure, the distribution of craft beer is limited by the existence of the restrictive three-tier distribution system

---

[7] What is a Beer Distributor? – *National Beer Wholesalers Association; nbwa.org*

and a beer market duopoly held by Anheuser-Busch/InBev and MillerCoors.

These laws have evolved over the years and what exists now is a unique mix of distribution laws that can easily confuse your team as it expands its market presence. There are three principal categories as follows:

- States that allow breweries to self-distribute without restriction
- States that prohibit craft brewers from any form of self-distribution
- States that permit self-distribution only up to a certain volume

In addition, you may discover that some states also have franchise laws that further regulate the relationship between distributors and breweries. These laws allow the brewery to sell to a distributor the exclusive right to distribute that brewery's beer in a specified geographic area.

This poses little concern for you while a startup with minimal sales volume as the franchise right has no value. However, as your brewery gains traction and dramatically increases its sales, that right appreciates in value. Down the road, this could result in your wanting to make a change in representation if the distributor is not making a reasonable effort to sell your beer. This can lead to a protracted negotiation to exit a current distribution agreement in favor of a new partner more committed and aligned with promoting your craft brewery over the long term.

Thus, the industry structure can be very limiting to distributing a craft brewery's products. Furthermore, not only do breweries have to deal with navigating the complex maze of distribution laws whenever they want to expand their geographic reach, but they must also deal with market pressures that make distribution unattractive.

Reaching distribution agreements can be a time consuming and ultimately frustrating process. Currently, two "mega brewers" (AB In-Bev/SAB Miller & Molson/Coors) largely control up to 80% of volume in the marketplace. Often these wholesaler's first priority is to promote their in-house brands that may also include well-known craft labels. An example of this is Molson/Coors who also owns Blue Moon as a subsidiary.

Indeed, it is difficult to assess whether a third party company will take the same special care of your "new baby" out in the marketplace. In general, there may be several smaller firms available as alternatives within a designated selling area (i.e. county boundary). Your team will need to assess which distributor will support your brewery's initial introduction to a market and on-going strategic and tactical execution capabilities.

While possible to make a switch in distributors it can be very expensive and disruptive to a growing business. I would advise that you spend time up-front to conduct due diligence (i.e. checking references, speaking to existing clients, visiting the market) to ensure you are making an informed decision before proceeding.

The recent consolidation in the beer industry is indeed increasing the pressure on distributors to focus on these macro breweries. Miller and Coors entered a joint venture in 2006 and InBev purchased Anheuser-Busch in 2008 for $52 billion.

In 2016 Anheuser-Busch InBev, closed on its more than $100 billion acquisition of rival SABMiller creating the world's largest brewer. The combined company has a staggering $55 billion in annual sales and an estimated global market share of 28 percent. The new firm, in order to receive regulatory approval in the U.S., SABMiller gave up ownership of the Miller brands by selling its 58 percent stake in MillerCoors to Molson Coors for $12 billion.[8] With the latest sale, A-B InBev's U.S. market share remains at about 45 percent.

Where Does It All Lead?

I have given you an amazing amount of information in this chapter. I imagine you are feeling like the data is coming at you from the end of a fire hose on full blast!

---

[8] AB/InBev finalizes $100B billion acquisition of SABMiller – Lisa Brown; *chicagotribune.com*, October 11, 2016

No doubt, it has taken months to convince family, friends, colleagues, angel investors and private equity firms to commit cash to your vision. The other critical decision is how best to distribute your product (directly or through a three-tier system) so your craft beer will get the shelf space and market penetration you desire.

I hope that you are now "fired up and ready to go" forward with your dream! It will take lots of hard work, and determination on your part, and many long hours of dedicated time put in at your brewery, but it will most definitely be worth it to take the plunge! **The next chapter will change our focus to the marketing and branding side of building a profitable craft brewing business.**

Chapter Six

Becoming a Pink Flamingo

Currently, there are over 6,000 craft breweries and brew pubs in the United States (through the end of 2017) with the number continuing to grow. I suspect that it has taken a lot longer than you originally anticipated to name your brewery, partially due to the number of new craft breweries coming on-line every year   Eventually, you will find that a lot of your ideal names may already have been claimed.

This chapter is a simple primer on how to create a memorable brand name, logo and unique packaging approach for your new craft brewery. I am going to spend some time discussing an approach that makes sure no other aspiring brewers have hijacked your vision and how you can trademark your exciting beer names. I will also share some practical examples on how merchandising, the proper use of social media, and mug clubs, can bring incremental revenue to your business and reinforce your overall brand image in a positive fashion.

Celebrating the Pink Flamingo Story!

A critical element in building a successful craft brewery is the ability to consistently connect with your primary audience. This can be all the local folks that come to your tasting room on a Friday evening for a quick pint and camaraderie to kickoff the weekend. Alternatively, it may be those beer geeks (I know I am one) that chase down gold medal winning drafts they have only read about on rating sites like the Beer Advocate found at (www.beeradvocate.com), Rate Beer (www.ratebeer.com) or Untappd (www.untappd.com). No matter the age or stage in life of your customers, it helps to have a hook that draws everyone to your doors.

Thus, I encourage my clients to have a story that resonates with both your team and the hometown tasters that will become your ambassadors out in the local marketplace. Being able to tell a great tale brings meaning to your endeavor of brewing and to you selling the best beer around.

Let me share a recent story from **Tim Klatt** at Strange Land Brewery in Austin (TX) to illustrate my point. He shared with me the power of honoring a "local legend". The site where they built their new brewery facility had previously been an outdoor gardening center. It was well known that a signature icon for the prior owner was to place plastic pink flamingos all around its perimeter. This unusual display quickly caught the attention of the local Austin authorities who sued to have the birds removed as a public nuisance.

Meanwhile, the owner put forth that he was just exercising his right to a public art display on his private property. The case ultimately was sent to the Texas high court that ruled in favor of the garden center. Meanwhile, everyone around Austin knows the story of Pink Flamingo corner on the west side of town.

Thus, when Tim and his partner Adam finally decided to launch a new IPA in 2017 they thought using the Flamingo as the new beer's name was a perfect tie-in to their locally focused identity. In fact, this wonderful brew is anticipated to shortly become their most popular offering. The value added to their "brand" is significant and measurable, setting the brewery up for long-term success in a very competitive market.

So how do you create a brand presence for your Brewery? Your company's brand is more than just its logo. In fact, it serves a greater purpose highlighting what image your brewery projects outwardly to the community. It clearly shows both potential clients and consumers what your team cares about, what you value in life, and what "friends" can expect from your beer.

The brand also sets your brewery apart from the many competitors that also brew a great IPA or memorable Siason. It tells your audience why they should pick up your latest product and not someone else's. I believe Jeff Bezos aptly summarized it when he said, "Your brand is what people say about you when you're not in the room."[1]

---

[1] Benefits of a Strong Brand Presence and How to Achieve One – Jaime Nacach; *Bloominari.com*, March 5, 2016

You will find that having a strong brand presence will make a significant difference for your craft brewery no matter the size or location. Specifically, it can help your team gain traction in the local marketplace for your expanding business in the following ways:

- Build and grow your reputation
- Stand out and apart from competitors
- Convey stability
- Positively influence potential customer's purchasing decisions
- Acquire new customers easier
- Construct loyalty and trust

How to Achieve A Stronger Brand Presence

In general, brand presence and awareness is often measured by how well a consumer can identify and connect with both your brand and company. Here are some key strategies your team may want to utilize in creating a stronger brand presence:

First, focus on your target audience, as most likely, your beer isn't perfectly suited for everyone. As such, you should know and have a deep understanding of the concerns, needs, preference, and lifestyle specific to your target audience.

Research has shown that a majority of craft beer enthusiasts and drinkers, but not all, are males between the ages of 35 to 49 years old. Completely understanding this can also help you give them the information they want and need in a way they will understand it. This can also help raise the personal connection between your brand and the consumer, whether they are sitting in your tasting room or picking up a six-pack at the local package store.

I have included below an infographic [2] that provides some additional insight into the craft beer drinker to kick-start your research.

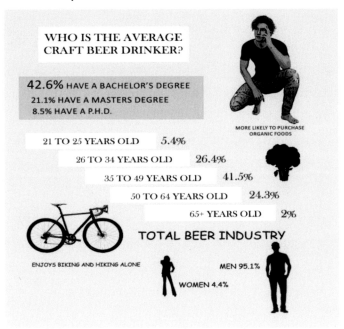

Second, create a personal connection between your brand and the craft beer drinker. One of the key pillars to building and maintaining a successful brand presence is to develop a strong level of trust between your brewery and your end-user.

Maintaining impeccable customer service and speaking to your audience in a way they will respond to, not just the way you want to say something, can help this level of trust grow. Furthermore, you as the craft brewer can heighten this connection through a vibrant on-site tasting room operation and selling merchandise to your visitors.

Third, it is critical to remain consistent with the image your team has created for your brewery or brew pub operation. How you present your brand should be clear across all channels and to anyone that comes into contact with it. Your branding should be integrated into every aspect of the firm including website, social media, advertising, point of sale flyers and other marketing material thus maintaining a strong presence. If your brand doesn't remain consistent, it can create confusion, slow down or disrupt the buying process, or even lead to your potential beer buddy choosing a competitor.

I will share another real life example to further illustrate my point. While out to dinner with my family the other night I noticed a couple at a table near ours. The young dude spent a good deal of the night texting on his cell phone. I couldn't imagine what was so important that it could not wait until after dinner, but I did notice that his female companion seemed very agitated by the situation. I imagine she felt ignored, unimportant, barely noticed, like she was simply taking up space at the table.

Witnessing this event got me thinking about brands and how so many simply take up space on the shelf, ignored and barely noticed. This is especially true with craft beers where there is always a hot new style or flavor of the month attracting attention.

Sure, craft drinkers may be aware of the brand. They know it exists and have probably seen a commercial or two for it. They may even "take it out on a date" if it's on sale or their usual brand isn't available. However, while drinking the beer, the individual may be thinking of their usual brand; the one on which they would rather spend their money.

It's not enough for buyers to be aware of your brand. Awareness does not breed brand loyalty. It is most important to be top of mind in the consumer's thoughts and emotions when thinking of craft beer. Equally critical is having your product physically present, ready and able to be grabbed from the shelf at a moment's notice. Successful advertising breeds these concepts but only a physical connection seals the deal.

It's true many brewery names come from stories. Stories are good. Stories help build a brand. ParrotDog was founded by guys who owned a parrot and called each other 'Dog'. That's great. But stories are not what I want to talk about here. I'm more interested in the mechanics of what makes one brewery name work better than another.

A memorable name attracts customers and sells more beer. A crappy name discourages customers and will lose you sales. There are also quite a few pitfalls that new breweries can fall into when it comes to naming themselves and their beers.

Now I know what you're thinking and I totally agree: surely the quality of what's in the glass should be more important than what it says on the label. Yes, it should. But getting your beer into the hands of first-time customers is also important. You want your brewery name to stick in someone's head and, if your beer impresses them, you can create something valuable – a returning customer.

First, let me share a few examples of some unusual and exotic names I uncovered while researching this book.

"There's no place like Gnome" and "Take me Gnome tonight" are two popular phrases at Hopping Gnome Brewing Company in Wichita, Kansas. Owners Torrey and Stacy Lattin opened Hopping Gnome in 2015. The pair had several other names in mind, but after researching, they discovered that most names they liked were already taken or too similar to other established breweries across the US.

One night, Torrey found a small gnome in their home that was a giveaway from the 2012 Kansas City Royals All Star game. He was immediately inspired by his find and asked Stacy, "How about Hopping Gnome? You know, like hops, and gnomes are known for drinking."

A name like Hopping Gnome did the trick. The name stuck and after finding a local graphic designer to create the awesome logo, Hopping Gnome Brewing Company was born. Located in the up-and-coming Douglas Design District, Hopping Gnome Brewing Company joined the growing craft beer community as the first taproom in Wichita, KS.

They decided on a small taproom with a 5 BBL brewing system and distribution plan rather than a restaurant in order to create a beer-focused atmosphere, where friends can get together and play games, order in a pizza, and hang out like it's your friend's house. Loyal customers refer to the brewery as "The Gnome" and have found a home in this strange, gnome filled sanctuary.

Stacy recalls, "[Customers] will give us garden gnomes to display in the taproom as well as send us gnome t-shirt ideas. We try to include the gnome theme whenever we can without being too over the top." They even call their samplers "Gnome Pours" and blame the gnomes when the beer runs out.[3]

While some brewery names are created to fit the brewery, Funky Buddha fit their brewery to an already

---

[3] 9 Weird Brewery Names and the Stories Behind Them – Danele Bova; *craftbeer.com*, January 24, 2017

existing name. Owner Ryan Sentz rebranded his craft beer lounge and tea bar into what is now known as Funky Buddha Brewery. R & R Tea Bar, Sentz's first endeavor, began as a hookah lounge and tea bar. Later, he added a large selection of craft beers. As the R & R Tea Bar and Funky Buddha Lounge's popularity grew, Sentz realized his passion for homebrewing could morph into something more.

The culture of that original Funky Buddha Lounge expands into their beers and marketing. Funky Buddha Brewery creates unique, outside the box beers, utilizing interesting ingredients to achieve over-the-top flavors and aromas. Many of their beers create a flavor profile that mimics certain foods and leaves a lasting impression on craft beer fans, such as their Blood Orange IPA, Blueberry Cobbler Ale, Sweet Potato Casserole Strong Ale, Maple Bacon Coffee Porter and French Toast Double Brown Ale.

While what's inside the bottle may seem the most important element, the outer label also helps create a lasting impression. Funky Buddha's labels are bright and colorful, and often cartoonish. These labels aid in the overall experience when enjoying a Funky Buddha brew. This fast growing enterprise was acquired by Constellation Brands in August 2017 and added to a High End and Craft Specialty business line. It will be fascinating to see how the business grows in the future.

Should I Use Bottles or Cans for my Craft Brew?

A key decision for you and your brewery team is what type of packaging to use – bottles, cans or both. There are indeed different impressions and practical reasons out in the marketplace about which option is preferred by craft beer fans. It will also have a significant impact on your overall brand image..

Defying the age-old edict that says beer in bottles is the more flavorful way to go, beer makers large and small are increasingly turning to the canning method — to the point that canned beer has acquired something of a retro-chic status.

Here are some factors to consider as you chart your path forward. First, canned beer weighs less. Less packaging means you can move the same amount of product in fewer trips, reducing your expenses and carbon footprint at the same time.   Biking to the store? Grab cans over bottles. Tired of glass breaking in the cooler on your road trip? Cans are safer. Own a grocery store (or a refrigerator)? Cans are more stackable.

Second, nearly everyone can agree that **cans are much more practical than bottles**, especially for outdoor recreation. They don't shatter, never require an opener, weigh less, fit more handily into a cooler, and impact the environment less.   Canned beer also chills better, and **collective hysteria** over BPA poisoning — a chemical in the lining of aluminum and plastic products — has gone out of vogue.

Third, cans are **completely airtight and keep out all light**, therefore preventing the beer inside from becoming tainted. Where cans deliver the true haymaker is in their power over exposure to air. If the end goal is to make sure the beer in your hand tastes as fresh as possible from oxidation, cans have the leg up over bottles.

However, just because cans are fantastic for keeping crisp IPAs fresh doesn't mean they're the answer to every brewer's problems. In fact, there are numerous reasons your team may clearly choose bottles over cans. Some are purely technical while others are aesthetic. Some use the Belgian and French tradition of styles as a stepping off point.

In addition, about half of craft beer consumers say that cans impart a distinct metallic taste in the beer, and the other half say they taste no difference. Recently a study was conducted that analyzed the perceived taste difference in canned versus bottled beers. Researchers didn't detect any metallic taste in the canned beers, and found little to no taste differences between canned and bottled versions of each beer[4].

---

[4] How Beer in a Can Became Hot – Matt Clinch; *cnbc.com*, June 9, 2016

Meanwhile, as of 2012, cans constituted 53.2% of the beer market while bottles had a 36.5% share — a fairly significant gap. By contrast, in 2006, the two packages were much closer in popularity — cans accounted for 48.3% of the market and bottles 41.9%. Draft beer largely accounts for the rest of brew sales.

Recently, Anheuser-Busch unveiled a style-conscious 11.3-ounce bowtie can — it tapers inward at the middle — for its popular Budweiser brand (MillerCoors has a commemorative series of Miller High Life cans coming out this summer that pay homage to Harley-Davidson motorcycles).

And perhaps most significant, Samuel Adams has introduced what it bills as the Sam can, a container that's designed with such features as a larger opening and an extended lip — all of which are intended to bring out the beer's full flavor.

The move is creating buzz in the industry not only because of the time and investment involved — the Sam can took two years and $1 million-plus in research and development to create — but also because brewery founder Jim Koch had previously balked at the idea of going the canned route, despite pressure from the craft brewery's many fans.

It is this type of out of the box thinking that has made craft beer such an exciting business for your team.

Beer still is defined by its packaging and while canned beer is on the rise, bottled beer isn't going anywhere.

How Do I Protect My New Brand?

Whether your new enterprise is based on a city, animal, plant, mythical creature, family name, embarrassing incident or other idea you now will need to make sure your new "brand name" is properly protected.

Clearly, you've got a lot on your mind to get your brewery operation up and running. The range of challenges and associated details can seem overwhelming to you and your team. Typical questions that may arise include those about financing, federal and state licensing, recipe formulation, hop contracts, distribution, employees and a thousand other things. **One area that is frequently overlooked by both new and experienced brewers is the issue of federal trademark registration.**

No doubt it is easier to focus on new equipment purchases such as fermenters, bright tanks and keg fillers. Nevertheless, your most important piece of property is ultimately your brand, and the primary expression of that identity is a trademark. The combination of your unique (hopefully) brewery name, individual beer identities, and logos are the day-to-day link between your craft brew and your end users.

So imagine that you receive a cease and desist letter and you're forced to change your brewery or beer name, even after years of use, and all of a sudden your customers aren't able to make that link. This can be a devastating blow to a brewery, and it is happening more these days. There are over 6,000 breweries in America and there are only so many brewery/beer names out there.

A federal trademark is your best (though not an absolute) defense against such a trademark conflict. But there are other benefits to federal trademark registration as well including the following:

- Nationwide notice of ownership of the mark and nationwide priority of use. In other words, your brewery's right to use the trademark, and to exclude others from using the trademark, extends to all 50 states even if you haven't sold beer there.
- Protects against the subsequent federal registration by others of confusingly similar names. Thus, if another brewery were to try to register a trademark for your brewery's name or beer name, the United States Patent and Trademark Office would prevent them from doing so.
- Serves as evidence of the validity and exclusive ownership of your mark at trial.
- Allows you to use the ® symbol, which puts others on notice of your federal registration.
- Grants the right to file a trademark infringement action in federal court, which provides different and better recovery options than a suit in state court.
- Deters others from using or applying for your trademark.

So what are your next steps in obtaining a federal trademark distinction for your new brewery? First, conduct a proper trademark search before deciding on a final brewery name or various beer names. This process should include visiting the very useful U.S. Patent & Trademark Office website which can be found on the web at **http://www.uspto.gov/trademarks/index.jsp**, and then clicking on "TESS search trademarks." From there, your team can run different types of searches with variables such as trademark name, goods and services.

Searching for a trademark isn't as simple as just typing in the trademark and submitting a query. For instance, if you want to make a **Red Street IPA**, simply searching **RED STREET IPA** or even **RED STREET** and looking for registered marks claiming beer often won't be enough. For example, **REDD STREET, RED ROAD, and RAD STREET** for beer could all pose problems. A thorough clearance will most often consist of multiple searches with different variables and phonetic variations.

Even when the initial trademark investigation is clear, you should go the extra step and perform searches with different variables for "common law" uses of the trademark in commerce. The reason for this is that even if you are able to register a trademark, if there is a senior/prior user of the mark (even if unregistered), that party may have superior rights to the trademark in the area where they used the mark prior to your registration. While proper trademark searches can be complicated, they are a good idea and should be contemplated whenever a new brewery or beer is being named.[5]

Second, apply for and obtain federal trademark registrations, preferably on an intent-to-use filing basis.[6] There are three key reasons why an application for a federal trademark can be rejected. When naming your brewery and beers, it is a good idea to use terms that are not merely descriptive of beer, geographically descriptive, or primarily a surname. In simpler terms, an application may be rejected if your mark is too close to another registered or previously applied for mark, when taking into account a number of other factors including how similar the goods or services are to each other.

---

[5] Choosing Your Brewery Beer Names and Trademark Searching – Brendan Palfreyman; *newyorkcraftbeer.com*, January 5, 2015

[6] The Importance of Trademark Registration for Brewers – Brendan Palfreyman; *newyorkcraftbeer.com*, December 1, 2014

What Purpose Does Branded Merchandise Serve?

This chapter has largely focused on the critical element of building an easily recognized and memorable brand for your brewery. A core part of the experience that visitors, guests, friends and colleagues receive when visiting your tasting room. This is where your team can put its best foot forward without having any outside competition.

This is also the portion of your on-site business where you can make a lasting positive impression. The combination of a fun and informative brewery tour coupled with tasting your great beer will create special memories and a dedicated following. That is exactly the time to have innovative branded merchandise such as t-shirts, hoodies, baseball caps and pint glasses. You will have a captive audience that wants to take home a growler or two of your latest offering and a souvenir to remember the trip!

These are easy and profitable sales once you have an infrastructure established to supply these goodies. The margins on these items usually averages 40% without any advertising needed. In addition, all your patrons instantly become brand ambassadors for your brewery as they walk around their hometowns extolling the virtue of your beer. Getting pictures of these customers wearing your branded merchandise is also ideal content for your social media tie-ins and special event promotions.

Overall, the tasting room operation is that hidden gem that can be your greatest moneymaker! A keg of beer sold in your tasting room generates seven (7X) times the revenue received from selling through a distributor. Having high quality food readily available adds to the full experience a client receives. And having branded merchandise available increases your overall margins while offering your customers something fun to wear or bring home from their enjoyable time at your brewery. It also reinforces the message that your brewery or brew pub distinguishes itself as truly unique when compared to others in your same geographic market.

Chapter Seven

Where No Man Has Gone Before!

I have always been a huge Star Trek fan. I loved the adventures of the USS Enterprise as it "boldly goes where no man has gone before" navigating new worlds and new civilizations. It was always clear that Captain Kirk, Spock and the crew were risk takers looking for new ways to solve unique problems.

The type of decision making required of accomplished brew masters in crafting new flavors and categories reminds me of the Enterprise Crew making creative decisions and implementing innovative solutions.

You probably have a favorite episode whether from one of the various TV versions (Original, Next Generation, Deep Space Nine, Voyager, Enterprise or now Discovery) or adaptations for the movies. The excitement about the science fiction genre is that you can immerse yourself in a colorful world with endless possibilities limited only by your imagination.

Likewise, a key challenge for you is how to apply the spectrum of opportunities available today into your craft beer business so you can become an innovator in your industry.

This chapter will provide you with some insights on why it is so critical to keep your craft business fresh and distinctive in today's hyper-competitive marketplace. It is simply not sufficient to brew great beer unless there is a broader concept that keeps bringing customers back for more. In fact, your ability to innovate may quickly spell the difference between thriving and just hanging on in this exciting industry

What is Innovation?

Lets start with a brief description of what is innovation and how it is often experienced in the craft beer space. I checked some leading academic experts and found a few descriptions that seem appropriate for our needs[1]:

- *"**Creativity is thinking of something new. Innovation is the implementation of something new**" - Paul Sloane is a Speaker, Facilitator and Author, specializing in entertaining talks & workshops on creativity, lateral thinking & innovation*

- *"**Very simply put, innovation is about staying relevant**". We are in a time of unprecedented change. As a result, what may have helped an organization be successful in the past could potentially be the cause of their failure in the future" - Stephen Shapiro is an Innovation Instigator, Hall of Fame Speaker and Author.*

No doubt, the craft beer industry has become one of the most innovative industries in America. You, as brewers, blend tradition, regional tastes, and artistry to make some of the best beers in the world. Nothing defines the product of this industry more than the over 150 unique and different styles available. Furthermore, there is literally a beer for every season in the craft industry

---

[1]What is Innovation? 15 Innovation Experts give us their definition — *ideatovalue.com*, March 18, 2016

whether it's peach wheat, pumpkin porter or gingerbread ale.[2]

Furthermore, against all odds, you see the craft brewing business is booming in a regulatory environment setup for a different competitive landscape.[3] In fact, recent changes to alcohol laws are helping. Brewpubs, for example, were illegal in many places when craft brewing began to expand as a viable business, but now there's no shortage of them. The majority of states have also legalized the sale of beer with alcohol content greater than 3.2 percent thus expanding the product possibilities for the brewers. "If there's an ethos of the craft brewing industry it's that there are no rules, there are no limits to what we can do. If the beer tastes good, that's all that really matters," says Maureen Ogle, historian and author of *Ambitious Brew: The Story of American Beer*[4].

Why Does Innovation Matter?

So the lesson to take away is that breweries of all sizes must continue to bring new products and ideas forth. There are no consumers more responsible for the current

---

[2] There's No Stopping the Craft Beer Craze – Katie Nodjimbadem; *smithsonianmag.com*, October 23, 2015

[3]Brewing Better Law: Two Proposals To Encourage Innovation In America's Craft Beer Industry – Andrew D'Aversa; *scholarship.law.upenn.edu*, Volume 165

[4]There's No Stopping the Craft Beer Craze – Katie Nodjimbadem; *smithsonianmag.com*, October 23, 2015

success of the craft brewing industry than millennials. While this demographic of young adults seems to shoulder a disproportionate amount of scorn, the craft brewing industry understands the value of millennials as a consumer base.

Thus, you and your team will need to constantly develop new beers to satiate the consumer's (mostly millennial) thirst for the wild and crazy. However, beware that this can be costly for small brewers, but it's these beer connoisseurs that have made the industry what it is today.

Let me share a story I uncovered during my research for this book that brings the impact of innovation to a practical level. It is about a unique concept in the craft business at O.H.S.O. Brewery and Distillery in Phoenix. This team lead by Jon Lane have developed an unusual perspective on delivering craft beer to the local population. O.H.S.O. (Outrageous Homebrewers Social Outpost) is a restaurant, local nano-brewery, distillery, and dog-friendly social hot-spot.

Through a shared love of his city and the people who inhabit it, Jon has been able to create a successful business fueled by the strong customer loyalty he receives from his beer-loving patrons. A key component of this local focus is supporting non-profit organizations through the donation of beer and allowing the groups to create custom brews at the O.H.S.O. facility on its nano system.

In fact, O.H.S.O holds, on average, one event per week for charitable and non-profit organizations, and last year gave $120,000 back to the community. When you share your resources, whether it's directly to charities or through beer-centric events, you naturally build positive word-of-mouth promotion, which boosts customer retention and helps you draw in a new crowd year-round. And it's not just charities that can brew up a frosty cold beer.

The brewery offers a class where you can work with one of O.H.S.O.'s brewers to create an original flavor, which I am sure plays a pretty hefty role in building loyalty and boosting customer retention. After all, who doesn't want to learn how to make their own frothy brew? In addition, the brewery team has also developed an app that lets customers schedule a brewing class, or simply see what's on tap right now, putting convenience right at patrons' fingertips — another way to keep customer satisfaction levels overflowing.

Creatively Naming Your Brewery

You have made great progress, thus far, in pulling together your vision for an amazing craft brewery. The beer you are producing is the talk of the town with your friends and family urging you on to greatness. Meanwhile, you have figured out how much space and type of equipment needed to launch your dream. Concurrently, you have gathered some start-up capital from either a crowd funding pitch or through angel investors.

So now you face a critical question…how do you name your new Craft Beer? A key component that you should consider is how to create a distinctive brand that will be easily recognized. Your aim is to attract a large group of dedicated beer enthusiasts, friends, family and colleagues. In addition, you want to build a group of committed ambassadors to follow your journey on social media as well.

Indeed, creating a great name for your craft brewery is equally important to producing "award winning" beers. Just consider that there are now over 6,000 brew pubs, microbrewers and regional craft brewers around the U.S. through the end of 2017. Thus, It is critical you "dream up" a moniker that reflects your unique approach to life and why anyone else should care about your brand. Ultimately, the logo, beer names and packaging must all tie together in a cohesive package

This is a wonderful opportunity to share your team's background (e.g. who you are) and the quirky story and circumstances that brought you together. You can also let the real world, outside your immediate circle of friends, know what drives you passion (e.g. what you believe in) and how that is reflected in your new business. Finally, you want to let new consumers of your beers connect with your mission (e.g. what you stand for) as it may well align with their worldview. This is especially true of millennial aged drinkers who represent the largest segment of craft beer drinkers.

What's in a Name?

Ultimately, this upfront thinking will become the core for your brand identity, beer packaging, social media presence, marketing approach, tasting room vibe and overall culture. And if it isn't well thought out, it can dog you for years!

Remember that another brewery from across town or the other side of the country can sue you over naming rights. While these issues can often be resolved in a positive fashion, the required effort often can be very distracting, time consuming and expensive.

Thus, let's look at four key factors to keep in mind as you come up with your brewery's innovative name.

- **Available** - Clearly, the most critical element in naming your brewery, given all the competition, is whether your "perfect" idea has already been taken. Is there another brewery, winery, or distillery with the same (or similar) name? How about a similar beer name? Is your preferred website name (e.g. URL) available? How about social media handles?

The number of competitors can make this seem a daunting task for your squad. However, with the amount of Cease and Desist orders flying around, resolving these questions in advance is a must for naming any brewery forever more[5].

- **Likeable / Fun To Say** - Craft Brewing is all about having a good time as you sit around tasting new flavor combinations using innovative ingredients. In fact, like great beer, brewery names can be evaluated on their "mouth feel". Does the proposed name easily roll off your tongue?

Do you want to be tied to a physical location? Does the beer remind you of a mythical creature? Do you want to consider a name that rhymes or is irreverent? Many of these options may seem hard to quantify, yet a good name should indeed be fun to say. Furthermore, the subtle tie-in to your greater mission can often be an important element of well-planned brand strategy.

- **Easy To Spell/Memorable** - Think about your core customer who is walking into a local pub and looking at all of the many options on tap. It can be overwhelming as you try to remember the name of that new beer your friends told you about the other evening at a poker game.

---

[5] What Makes for A Great Brewery Name – CODO Design; craftbeerbrandingguide.com

So it is important that the brewery and beer names be easy to spell and recall. This doesn't necessarily mean that your preferred name has to be short, although that can be a great attribute as well. However, no matter the length, your name needs to be something people can easily pronounce.

- **Flexible/Portable** - Remember that you are expecting your craft brewery will ultimately grow to be a regional juggernaut selling over 15,000 barrels annually. Thus, you want to ensure the name you have chosen "translates" well once you expand into new markets.

While dreaming up the perfect moniker be careful to avoid a short-term fad or focus on a hyper-local theme. Will your brewery name lend itself to more expansive themed campaigns? Think about your flagship beers and how their names can further enhance your overall brand name and story.

Finally, be wary of using totally invented words in your name. Keep in mind that these often carry no special meaning to potential beer connoisseurs, making your team have to work harder to tell your story. Of course you will do this anyway through great branding and beer, but why start off in the hole if you can avoid it? You should also think about how well you name translates to foreign languages so you avoid offending anyone by accident!

Before I let you get rolling with that first brainstorming session pour yourself a frosty cold one. Now lets have a little fun as I give you a list of 20 randomly selected craft breweries and their "infamous" beer names from around the country. I hope the profiles will provide you with some inspiration for your naming process.

Brewery Name	**Beer Name**
Palo Alto Brewing Company	Hoppy Ending Pale Ale
Stone Brewing Company	Arrogant Bastard Ale
Russian River Brewing Company	Blind Pig IPA
21st Amendment Brewery	Brew Free! or Die IPA
New England Brewing Company	Gandhi-Bot
The Lost Abbey	Duck Duck Gooze
Epic Brewing Company	Hop Zombie
Ruckus Brewing Company	Hoptimus Prime
Foothills Brewing	Sexual Chocolate Imperial Stout
Ridgeway Brewing	Bad Elf
Brew Cult Brewing	Get Down American Brown
Mother's Brewing Company	Lil' Helper
Snake River Brewing	Zonker Stout
Wasatch Brewery	Polygamy Porter

Ferral Brewing Company	Barrique Okarma
Stoudts Brewing Company	Smooth Hoperator
Coney Island Brewing Company	Human Blockhead
Great Divide Brewing Company	Hibernation Ale
Four Peaks Brewing Company	Kilt Lifter
Beer Valley Brewing Company	Leafer Madness

Making Your Brewery Stand Out in the Crowd

The craft beer industry is rapidly changing and evolving as the competition among breweries continues to intensify. Thus, it is critical that your team develop a unique point of difference in marketing your beer and running your operations. Now we will turn to some ways that you can make your brewery stand out from the crowd and continue to experience double digit expansion even as other competitors suffer setbacks. The list is broken down as follows:

- **Ingredients -** You will find that craft brewers are increasingly selecting more and more unusual and unique component for their beers. These include fruit flavors (e.g. orange, grapefruit), spices (e.g. sage, nutmeg), peppers (e.g. jalapeno, habanero) and seafood (e.g. oysters, shrimp) for a few examples. There are also a variety of unusual flavors such as bacon, maple syrup, wine must, coffee and chocolate are also now finding a home.

111

Virtually, the sky is the limit in terms of choices, however, it takes wisdom and experience to pair these and other components into flavorful and drinkable beers.

- **Marketing** – The industry is quickly becoming saturated with over 6,000 craft breweries and brew pubs in existence. Thus, it has becoming increasingly important for you to distinguish your product with a theme that can appeal to a very precise targeted market (e.g. millennials, extreme sportsmen). This concept should be carried through all aspects of how your brewery is marketed to the outside world including labeling and merchandise design.

- **New Aging Vessels** – Craft breweries are now stepping into new territories with approaches beyond traditional stainless steel tank aging. You will find more teams using various types of barrels (e.g. whisky, sherry, oak) to produce aged beers that have unique character. This is following the example from the wine industry and scotch & bourbon whisky distillers that have been experimenting over many years. The result is often a special quaff that can be featured in addition to the normal core or seasonal beer lineup.

Chapter Eight

Do You Need to Raid Your Piggy Bank?

Now you are really rolling with a great product and excited about the potential for opening your own Craft Brewery. I suspect that you have a location in mind and a good idea of all the equipment and supplies you will need to become fully operational. However, that goal has raised a key question for you and your team.

How much money do I need to launch my brewery?

This chapter is a simple primer on assessing the amount of capital and cash resources needed so you can fulfill your dreams! I am going to spend some time providing a roadmap through basic budgeting and acquiring all of your initial equipment and supplies to start-up your brewery as well. I may well cover topics that you "know by heart", nevertheless it is always helpful to hear the message multiple times as you get rolling toward glory!

Where Do I Start My Quest?

Well a logical question is how to get started. **A good place to begin is by estimating the total amount of resources that you will likely need for your first two years of operations**. A major short fall for new entrepreneurs and craft brewers is not having enough cash on hand to sustain the business during lean times. It always takes longer to achieve market penetration and costs more than expected due to the changing nature of the craft brewing business.

A critical component for determining the fundamental building blocks of your new brewery is an **Operating Budget.** This document is also known as a Profit and Loss statement (P&L) or pro-forma projection. Among other things, it helps forecast where your brewery will be selling its products (e.g. package stores, restaurants, beer bars, tasting room) and generating income each month.

This month-by-month revenue breakdown shows the impact on decisions to either self-distribute your beer or use a traditional third party distributor. In addition, it helps measure performance in selling takeaway brews (e.g. 64oz growlers), branded merchandise and on-site special events.

Ultimately, it provides a roadmap on how you will build your craft brewery income stream over time. It also provides some critical insight on how widely your Session IPA can be found (outside your brewery) by your cadre of dedicated beer connoisseurs and their friends.

The budget also lays out the normal costs that your team will incur to operate a successful brewery. These costs can be broken down into two different "buckets" for ease of understanding. First, is a category known as **Cost of Goods Sold (COGS).** These expenses include all the components needed to produce your beer including raw materials (i.e. barley, hops, yeast), packaging components (e.g. bottles, cans, trays), freight/shipping charges, cleaning supplies and grain/rubbish removal.

An initial measure of your financial performance is known as the **Gross Margin (GM).** This represents the amount of money generated when the total cost of goods sold is subtracted from total revenues. The GM is measured on both an absolute dollar value basis and as a percentage of revenue. The most efficient craft breweries will generate gross margins in the 50% to 70% range. This is part of the financial attraction to this exciting industry segment.

In addition, you can assess how productive your brewery team is at securing high yield from each batch of lager, stout or IPA brewed. In general, a 20-barrel brewing system will generate between 17 barrels (70% yield) and 19 barrels (90% yield) each time it is used. The average yield you may attain at your craft brewery once you have been brewing your "recipes" for a period of time is likely between 80% and 85% efficiency. The key variables are what type of tasty beverage is being produced and whether the raw ingredients such as hops tend to "suck up" the excess amounts of liquid in the fermentation tank.

Second, the budget includes a range of expenses that you will incur to get your finished product distributed to various retail and wholesale outlets. These items can be broken down in to the following ten (10) key categories.

- **Staffing Cost** – A breakdown of all the payroll and associated costs for the brewery team. These expenses are usually split out by functional area (e.g. production, sales, marketing, etc.) and include the employee benefits, payroll taxes and service fees.

- **General & Administrative** – All the expenses associated with managing the breweries administrative functions. This will include items such as travel and entertainment expenses, dues, conferences, website maintenance and payroll service charges for instance.

- **Sales and Marketing** – All expenses related to promotion of your products in the local and regional marketplace. This covers items such as wholesaler sales promotion, public relations, special events, website redesign, social media, tap handles, point-of-sale materials, product description flyers and more.

- **Licenses and Permits** – All the various licenses required by local, state and federal agencies to operate a craft brewery. Since these are alcoholic beverages there are more stringent reporting requirements covered by this line item.

- **Equipment & Supplies** – All the rental equipment used within the brewery. This can include items such as forklifts, carbon dioxide & oxygen tanks and propane. In addition, it covers the materials need for ongoing repairs and maintenance.

- **Property/Facility Costs** – All of the expenses associated with operation of your brewery facility. Your real estate decision will ultimately impact how much beer can be produced, stored and delivered in an efficient manner. This area will include items such as monthly rent, utilities, snow removal, property taxes, repairs and maintenance costs.

- **Professional Fees** - The fees and reimbursables charged by external consultants to support the heavy lifting being accomplished by your brewery team. These services can include accounting, bookkeeping, tax preparation, graphic design, marketing strategy, operations assessments and fund raising support among many services.

- **Insurance** - All of the various types of insurance coverage needed to protect your new business. This will cover items such as property, casualty, auto, directors, general business, workmen's compensation and healthcare premiums.

- **Financing Costs** - The cost of borrowing funds to pay for your on-going business expansion. This is typically in the form of regular payments made to banks, angel investors, private equity firms or even state economic development agencies.

- **Income Taxes** – All taxes due to local, state and federal (e.g. IRS) agencies for earnings from your amazing business. There are also credits that can be carried forward for those early years of operations when profits may be small or a loss incurred.

What Does It All Mean For My Brewery?

When combined, the income less expense (net) will let you know how profitable (or not) your operation is projected to be in any specific month or year. More importantly, you will want to track how much cash is

117

brought into the brewery (e.g. sales) versus being used for various strategic and operational needs (i.e. burn rate).

Remember, that there will be a delay in timing between when product is sold to either a distributor or retail outlet and funds are remitted. The state and federal regulation of malt beverages will specify how quickly (typically within 30 days) payment must be made.

The **Cash Flow** statement helps you better understand how your brewery actually makes money! This will assist your team in determining a clear direction on whether to sell only wholesale, open up a tasting room, provide food service on-site, offer special event promotions or contract brew for other entities.

A key measure of your financial health is known as the **Net Margin (NM).** This represents the amount of money generated when total cost of goods sold is subtracted from total revenues. The NM is measured on both an absolute dollar value basis and as a percentage of revenue. The most efficient craft breweries will generate net margins in the 2% to 5% range. A portion of the range is based upon the size of the operation and its overall efficiency.

WHY DOES CRAFT BEER COST SO MUCH?

Take a look at this graphic to find out why…

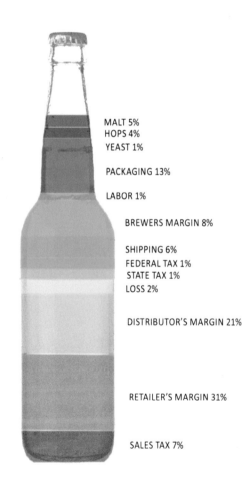

MALT 5%
HOPS 4%
YEAST 1%

PACKAGING 13%

LABOR 1%

BREWERS MARGIN 8%

SHIPPING 6%
FEDERAL TAX 1%
STATE TAX 1%
LOSS 2%

DISTRIBUTOR'S MARGIN 21%

RETAILER'S MARGIN 31%

SALES TAX 7%

Why Does Brewery Size Matter?

Since two "mega brewers" have now taken over the majority of US beer sales volume a key question you might ask is "does size matter" in designing your brewery operations. These large breweries (over 250,000 barrels annually) have developed a unique financial and performance model over a number of years focused on maximizing their economies of scale. This is the idea that when your brewery team produces a higher volume of a specific product it consistently drives the per unit cost lower. The "Big Beer" producers secure these results through bulk purchasing, large continuous batch production, automated processes, heat pasteurization, and years of perfecting their product and eliminating waste.

In general, these very large competitors expect to produce much higher operating margins then most craft brewers. In fact, you will see that these competitors created beers and their associated supply chains to help achieve this goal. According to Yahoo! Finance, Molson Coors' operating margin in 2014 was 12.33% and AB/In-Bev's (pre-merger) was an amazing 32.2%. This compares against the average operating margin for small, independent craft breweries of 2% in 2013[1].

---

[1] Are Craft Breweries Overpriced? — Mark Meckler; *craftingstrategy.com*, July 9, 2014

Unfortunately, the vast majority of craft brewers, like your new enterprise, do not have the cost advantages that inherently are realized with economies of scale. In addition, the unique blend of ingredients you utilize to create that special House Lager or Coffee Porter is all about developing a small batch customized brew versus controlling costs and increasing shelf life.

Nowadays, innovative brew masters demand high quality and often expensive ingredients that enhance the flavor and character of their latest creations. Moreover, the length and nature of your fermentation process can change dramatically with the style of beer being produced. A small batch of double dry hopped IPA, hand bottled and labeled, then delivered in a compact van does not meet the operating margin criteria for the big boys.

Nevertheless, this does help explain why local and regional craft brewers are able to maintain higher price points, yet these enterprises cannot keep the costs down like the mega brewers!

How Will Craft Brewers Thrive?

The mega brewers have the dominant share of the overall domestic beer market even with flat to negative growth trends. These entities will continue to look for craft breweries with great beers, memorable branding and a strong social media following. Many micro and regional brewers will discover unique opportunities to supercharge their business through mergers and JV arrangements with equal sized players. The resulting combined firms will have the ability to build more efficient operations and cover a broader distribution footprint.

Meanwhile, the craft marketplace is continuing to grow at nearly double-digit rates despite the number of new entries in every state around the U.S. In fact, you will quickly discover that America's craft breweries are strong, becoming more adaptable and smarter about business, every day. The push for innovation is spreading world wide as brew masters are offering customers products and services of real value.

Both you and I certainly recognize that the craft beer industry is a different animal. Rather than an addiction to efficiency, craft beer entrepreneurs are willing to accept lower profits and less streamlined processes. This is pursued in exchange for a better work/life balance, improved wages and health benefits for team members and raising everyone's overall happiness. This is possible simply because your typical craft beer drinker is willing to pay a higher price for a pint or a six-pack of good craft beer. In this case of craft, they are not engrossed with bargain seeking.

The chief reason for less price sensitivity is because overall the beer is truly superior, and because they love the movement and the ethic behind it. Perhaps it is a love of standing in line for the latest limited edition brew knowing that even with that high price, craft brewers are not ripping them off.

Nevertheless, there will come a time in the not too distant future when the number of craft breweries in operation will reach a tipping point. This is the time when you and I will start to see a further consolidation in the industry. Those enterprises that are only marginally profitable will likely start looking to cash out or find a strategic partner to improve their operational efficiency.

Indeed, the latest indication that craft beer is changing the rules came from the last place you might natural expect – Private Equity Investors. Recently, a number of high profile craft brewery founders were able to cash out and still maintain control of decision-making under a new ownership structure. The net effect was to allow the dynamic team that built the business to remain in place and ensure that the brand identity, beer quality and authenticity continued to draw new fans and beer drinkers.

How Do I Project My Cash Needs?

This is intended to provide you with a dose of reality about the requirements needed to get a medium sized microbrewery up and running. The craft beer business requires significant investment in material and equipment to grow and ultimately build a profitable brewery. It gives your team a working budget for both capital investments and operating capital.

Your team will need to determine how much capital investment is needed for the brewery start-up. This would include all of the equipment to be able to brew beer on a large-scale basis including brew kettles, fermenters, bright tasks, canning or bottle lines, keg fillers and numerous other elements. The landlord also has additional space adjacent to your leased space available for expansion when your brewery is ready.

Your team has decided to initially rent its space from a local landlord and then invest $40.00 per square foot ($400,000) in modifying the facility to meet your specific requirements. This includes adding key components for a properly functioning brewery including, but not limited to, the following major items:

- Brewing Facility
- ADA Bathrooms
- Tables and Chairs for Tasting Room
- Bar/Serving Area
- Security System
- Entertainment System
- Office Space
- Computers
- Merchandise Area with Displays
- Equipment Storage

Initially, there will be no dedicated food service offered on-site. Instead, customers, visitors and tourists can select different and unique options from food trucks and local restaurants in the immediate area that deliver. The tasting room will be large enough to accommodate parties and special events that energize and engage your regular fans. In addition, there will be a dedicated area for displaying and selling Golden Pup Brewery merchandise. The range of offerings includes t-shirts, hoodies, glassware, growlers, hats and other themed items.

A summary of the $1.1 MM+ estimated capital investment is outlined below. I also recommend that you include a 15% contingency factor for unanticipated changes to your original construction and build out plans. This project includes a detailed list of components for the Golden Pup Brewery as follows:

Brewery Equipment
3 Vessel15 Barrel Brewhouse System
- LauterTun/Kettle/Whirlpool with platform and piping
- Product Heat Exchange (chiller)
- Main control panel with 3 variable frequency drives
- 4 flow meters

Grain Handling
- Malt mill/grist hopper/flex auger delivery system

Water Systems
- Hot Liquor Tank/Cold Liquor Tank
- Pumps and piping, heater/chiller, temp probes

Brewery Accessories
- Wort line heat exchanger (hot sani)
- CIP pump, mash oar, mash hoe, din wrench, gaskets, clamps

Installation
Fermenters, Bright Tanks, Serving Tanks

- 6 – 30 barrel fermenters (jacketed)
- 2 – 30 barrel bright beer tanks (jacketed)
- 5 – 7 barrel single wall serving tanks
- Includes all required fittings, valves, carbonation assemblies, sample valves, pressure gauges, etc.

Hoses (Multiple sizes)

Miscellaneous Hardware
Brewery Rack System
Kegs (1/6 & ½ barrel)
Keg Washing Machine
Walk-in Refrigerator
Steam Boiler
Glycol Chiller
Forklift
Pallet Jack

A summary of the approximate $1.1 MM estimated capital investment is highlighted below:

In addition, there is regular operating capital that your new brewery will need to get up and running. This cash flow is needed to pay pre-opening salaries, insurance premiums, deposits, legal and accounting fees among other categories. This initial forecast assumes that you as the entrepreneur are not drawing a salary for this business initially. Once your brewery is up and running and have reached profitability there is more flexibility to pay yourself. The salaries are for critical team members including a brewmaster, tasting room staff and bookkeeper. **In general, having a six month cushion of cash resources will help smooth over the inevitable bumps in the road as your get your brewery operation running smoothly.** A simulated breakdown is as follows.

FIXED ASSETS	AMOUNT
Real Estate-Land	N/A
Real Estate-Buildings	N/A
Leasehold Improvements	$400,000
Equipment	$560,000
Furniture and Fixtures	$40,000
Contingency (15%)	$150,000
Other	
TOTAL FIXED ASSETS	**$1,150,000**

OPERATING CAPITAL	AMOUNT
Pre-Opening Salaries and Wages	**$125,000**
Prepaid Insurance Premiums	**$3,500**
Inventory	**$10,000**
Legal and Accounting Fees	**$5,000**
Rent Deposits	
Utility Deposits	**$2,000**
Supplies	**$12,000**
Advertising and Promotions	**$15,000**
Licenses	**$2,500**
Other Initial Start-Up Costs	
Working Capital (Cash on Hand)	**$75,000**
Total Operating Capital	**$250,000**
TOTAL REQUIRED FUNDS	**$1,400,000**

There are a number of different strategies that can reduce the upfront costs your team will need to incur. An example is to buy some gently used equipment from another craft brewer that has expanded its production facility to larger units (e.g. acquires 30 barrel brewhouse and sells a 15 barrel unit).

A second option to consider is initially leasing a facility for your new brew pub or craft brewery and then transition to owning a building as the business expands profitably.

I will go into greater detail about how such deals can be put together in our next chapter. In addition, we will spend time discussing where you might turn to raise the levels of funding necessary to make your craft brewery dream a reality.

Chapter Nine

Finding the Cash Cow!

So the stars are rapidly aligning for your brewery team! You have a fabulous group of brews that have been taste tested in the local marketplace to great acclaim. In addition, you have finally selected a unique name for your brewery unlike any other craft brewer in the country.

Your team is now excited about picking beer names and designing eye-catching graphics for your first canning production run. Finally, you have scoped out the location, core equipment needed and estimated total investment required for your initial operation. The key question you are probably asking yourself right now is **where and how do I get the money needed to launch my new craft brewery?**

A great place to start this discussion is by sharing the success story of a 20-year-old craft brewery – **Four Peaks Brewing Company** from Arizona. Back in 1996 the industry was just getting rolling (1,150 total breweries) and craft beer was not a well-known commodity. A number of industry insiders referred to this new beverage trend as "microbrews" not knowing how else to describe the unique mix of hops, yeast and malted barley.

Four Peaks was the brainchild of Andy Ingram who experienced the dynamic English beer and pub scene while studying overseas and returned with a vision to bring a similar experience to the US. Ingram started as an assistant brewer at a historic local brewery in Phoenix, under the tutelage of Clark Nelson. They shared their ideas and dreams of opening their own place. Around the same time, another group of more seasoned businessmen were also planning to open a brewery. The two parties crossed paths and eventually decided to collaborate.

The initial challenge was when they found an old dairy building on Eighth Street in Tempe, then a rundown part of the city. In a leap of faith, the partners signed a lease for the property before they had actually secured the required financing.

Unexpectedly, It turned out there was a lien on the property and the bank would not underwrite the loan. So where were they going to find the cash for funding their new brewery? Determined to find a way to get "rolling" the team quickly realized they needed a "Plan B".

During that early period of craft brewing numerous start-up breweries around the country needed equipment for building their breweries. The Four Peaks team saw this as an opportunity to make some money and started selling Grundy tanks from England (small, stainless steel vessels used for fermenting beer) to other breweries around the country.

The original working name of Cactus Creek Brewing Company didn't excite the partners. After discussing hundreds of monikers, they voted secretly on paper. "Though no one had Four Peaks as their No. 1 choice, the name was the only one to appear on all the ballots," Ingram recalls. And with that a new brewery was born. Finally, using the proceeds from the tank sales along with financing from friends and family in hand, things were a go for the Four Peaks team.

Though the business plan called for a full-service restaurant and bar, finances limited that idea to a production brewery. A few years later, an angel investor's funding provided the green light to fulfill that original vision.

After establishing itself with beers distributed into the Arizona marketplace via bars and liquor stores, the focus shifted toward turning the production facility into a full blown brewpub. The success of the original location created demand for a second full-service restaurant in Scottsdale and later a third at Phoenix Sky Harbor International Airport. The Wilson Road production facility, necessitated by the ever increasing demand for its

132

beer statewide, appeared and was equipped with a spacious tasting room.

Back in 2015, the partners were looking to expand the reach of the brand and business to a wider audience and realized the need for a strategic partner. Subsequently, Four Peaks was acquired in late 2015 by Anheuser-Busch InBev (ABI).

Despite initial backlash within the brewing community, Four Peaks weathered the storm and remains strong, thanks to the original ownership group's well managed day-to-day operations. The owners saw their hard work pay off and now these amazing beers can be enjoyed beyond the borders of Arizona. "It's been an amazing wild ride," said Andy Ingram.

How do I get started finding money?

I have found a number of resources available for you to get rolling with your brewery dreams. This chapter looks at a variety of places where you might secure the money you need throughout the life cycle of your business. Some options (e.g. friends and family) work better for smaller start-up enterprises while others (e.g. private equity firms) are better aligned with established and fast growing breweries.

The craft brewery business is especially capital intensive. Let me give you an example to put this in perspective. Let's say that your team is planning to start by brewing on a 3-barrel "nano" system and self-distribute draft beer only to local bars and restaurants. This has the positive impact of limiting the amount of capital needed "out of the gate" for equipment.

However, as your beer quickly becomes a local favorite and suddenly is in great demand more money will be required. You will need to rapidly expand your brewery's production by adding fermenters and even add a larger brew kettle. A unique challenge facing brewers is that you must build excess capacity ahead of actual marketplace demand. This is primarily due to the nature of the brewing equipment and tanks, which requires upfront capital expenditures and can have long lead times for delivery.

The net result is increased overhead expenses relative to the production volume. In simple terms this means you must often settle for a reduced profit margin on each case, log or barrel of craft beer you sell and must continue reinvesting in your growing brewery. Remember, that it will always require far more funding than you and your team originally anticipated to truly build a "world-class" brewing facility. **Whether you plan to offer only draft beer, distribute bottles and cans or have a tasting room allot a minimum 30% contingency for "scope changes".**

So if you have a rough breakdown of the cash requirements for your Nano system here is how that math might pan out for your team.

Brewery Equipment	$500,000
Materials & Supplies	$150,000
Working Capital	$100,000
Subtotal – Base Funding	$750,000
Contingency (30%)	$225,000
Total – Required Capital	**$975,000**

There is nothing worse than an undercapitalized business where you are always scrambling to make ends meet and pay the bills.   No doubt, unexpected circumstances will pop up from time to time where you have little control (e.g. tax bills).

You will also face on-going challenges about how to invest limited resources to make sure sales rapidly expand at your targeted double digit growth rate (e.g. 20% or more annually). You will find continuous tradeoffs between short-term returns via spending on brand marketing (e.g. social media, special events) and long-term capacity building (e.g. new fermenters).

What is Your Success Plan?

Clearly, year after year craft beer fans keep demanding new and varied tastes from their favorite brewery. You and your fellow craft brewers around the country are challenged to expand brewing capacity, build new facilities, distribute in new markets and increase innovation to meet this evolving demand.

This means that new investment and funding opportunities are suddenly available that previously did not exist, as Investors become even more enamored with this industry segment. Just think how much fun is it for you and your buddies to tell everyone that you "own a brewery"!

The available investment options vary widely so both new and experienced brewers looking to expand must first carefully consider their existing operations and their long-term goals. In fact, thanks to the rapidly expanding "love affair" between consumers and craft brewers, more Initial Public Offerings (IPO) and Merger & Acquisition (M&A) deals will continue in this industry.

You will quickly discover that once your brewery is fully operational and expands its revenue or volume, the existing processes and procedures often must be changed for greater efficiency. This is particularly true for craft breweries that draw a great following because their product is unique and limited to smaller batches.

Simultaneously, you are going to find that beer connoisseurs expect continuous innovation in the craft segment. Thus you and your team must work even more diligently to maintain and grow customer loyalty with new, diverse and tasty product introductions.

In this dynamic industry, brewers must be able to articulate both their short-term and long-term priorities, through their business model, to the investment community. For example, your short-term priority may be to expand the tasting room hours, increase your social media presence or introduce your newest German Kolsch to more customers and gain more local market share. In the long-term, the focus could be to increase the number of tanks at your brewery, or even build a new brewery in a new market, to keep up with demand.

There is a real opportunity to make "big" money in this rapidly changing field, however, it is critical you are well positioned to take advantage of the changes to come. Your own unique business model carries a different "risk profile" from even a similar sized craft brewer across town. For instance, your team may place its primary focus on being distributed within a 30-mile radius to ensure optimal freshness of your beers for thirsty drinkers.

A competitor, looking to grow rapidly, can team with third-party distributors in neighboring cities and states. Meanwhile, there are also numerous examples of larger breweries (over 15,000 barrels annually) that focus on brewing for other teams (e.g. contract brewing) more efficiently and at a lower overall cost.

Once your growth strategy is articulated, you can properly answer investor inquiries about existing and future operations and determining sources of funding.

Your strategic approach usually leads to a number of questions about capital expenditures and steps for operational improvement.

When setting up your business here are some key questions to consider among your team and potential "funders".

- Should you borrow money or have interested parties become "owners"?
- How are the long-term desires and expectations of your founding team matched with outside investors?
- Will your team be able to "afford" paying back a loan during the lean years following startup?
- What is the real cost of the capital and can it be reduced as the business grows?
- If there are equity partners, are they expecting cash and when?
- What is the exit strategy for your team and investors to ultimately "cash out"?

Different types of investors expect varying returns on their investment. For instance, equity investors do not usually require immediate repayment because they are investing in your company's long-term brand and earning potential. Nevertheless, you will discover these individuals or firms do expect higher returns on their investment. These returns can come as distributions to shareholders, as buyouts by other investors or through the sale of the company.

In exchange for this, equity investors often require a "voice" in your key business decisions, either formally or informally, to protect and ensure the maximum returns on their cash infusion. Furthermore, as the craft industry continues to mature it is now drawing more institutional equity investors, such as private equity funds and family offices. These sophisticated entities are now investing in craft brewers to provide growth capital and acquisition platforms.

Which Funding Source is Best for My Brewery?

So what does this all mean for you and your "band of brothers" as you jump into the craft beer business? I am going to take you on a short tour of some options you may want to consider as you build your brewery. I am generally placing them in order from easiest to attain up through the most complex.

A portion of that classification is dependent upon how large a business you actually plan to build when searching for money. I know from experience it is a very different conversation if you are a brewpub producing 1,500 annual barrels versus a Regional Brewery with over 20,000 barrels per year.

The individuals, groups, banks, finance companies, angel investors and private equity firms all have different motivations in backing your specific enterprise. It could be they are beer lovers and really appreciate the amazing Grapefruit IPA or Nut Brown Ale you are producing. They may think it is "totally cool" to be an owner of a craft brewery even if it just means getting discounted beer in the tasting room each weekend.

Alternatively, a more sophisticated investor may see your brewery as having a special lifestyle "feel" that can be grown into a national brand. Your rapidly expanding presence in new underserved markets may well fit into a broader strategy to acquire strong mid-sized regional players in creating a conglomerate to take on "Big Beer".

No matter what unusual story you bring forth, here is an initial list of potential capital sources. I have listed them in order of attractiveness based upon your role as the business founder. The financing options range from the simplest solution to the most complex.

I have determined this breakdown largely based on the amount of your business (e.g. equity stake) that an investor will require in exchange for writing a check. If you have ever watched Shark Tank this is where the entrepreneurs exchange a large chunk of their "baby" (e.g. 40%) for an essential capital infusion (e.g. $1.0 MM). You should remember that every deal is negotiable and that you want to maintain more than 50% of your business in friendly hands to ensure the brewery follows your vision. So let's get going with your options.

I. **Friends and Family Network** – *So Who you Gonna Call?*

This group represents your "true believers" who tasted that early, somewhat funky, home brew version yet still are sticking around for more. They have seen your evolution from a neophyte to a polished brew master with some truly exceptional beers.

Clearly, this is the most popular and logical group for start-up brewers seeking initial capital. You will need to spend time chatting with those that know you best, show your natural charisma and ultimately talk folks out of their money!

First you will need to know exactly what you are after in both total dollars and type of investment. Do you simply want a loan, or are you offering your family member a stake in your business for their investment?

The less business acumen your potential lender has, the more likely it is that you'll want a loan. Even though you're asking for a cash infusion from people you know doesn't mean you are any less professional. Thus you should plan to share an overview of your well-crafted business plan with family and friends.[2]

<u>Benefits</u>

- *Flexibility* – Ability to negotiate attractive terms with people who care deeply about your success

---

[2] Dos and Don'ts of Asking Family and Friends for Startup Funds? – Tony Armstrong; *nerdwallet.com*, January 19, 2015

- *Lower Cost* – Investors willing to forgo higher interest rates for being part of a exciting and relatable business

Challenges

- *Business Risk* – A business that fails can impact both personal relationships and family finances

- *Repayment Terms* – Clearly documenting the amount borrowed, the interest rate, the proposed repayment schedule and how they are investing in your business (e.g. equity or loan)

- *Helpful Interference* – This early class of investor may be less sophisticated so be clear upfront about the risks and rewards of providing money.

II. **Home Equity Loan** – *Should I bet my house or condo on this beer?*

Once you have exhausted the built-in fan base it is time to look at other assets you own as options. Your home or other real estate holdings can be a good place to secure funding if you have built up substantial equity over time. You may find this a low stress pathway to needed capital with traditional business loans often difficult to obtain especially for start-up enterprises.

Now this may be a challenge for you as a millennial that has been enjoying the "fruits of life" and having not yet become a homeowner. This is a one time lump sum loan that is repaid monthly at a fixed rate, just like a regular mortgage. It's very

142

predictable because you'll have the same exact payments each month. [3]

Benefits

- *Lower Cost* – Home equity interest rates are typically much lower than those of business loans

- *Fast and Cheap* – No need to justify a business plan if you have sufficient equity in your home

- *Independence* – Avoid bringing in additional investors thus retaining 100% ownership

Challenges

- *Home Risk* – Defaulting on the loan *Capital Required* – Bank can shutoff loan if value of underlying home decreases and business delays may eclipse available assets

- *Repayment Terms* – Monthly payment can exceed then income business will generate immediately

III. **Retirement Accounts** – *What about saving for a rainy day?*

A readily accessible asset is your 401(k) or individual retirement account (IRAs). It is likely you have built a lovely "nest egg" over time that can be used to fund your brewery dreams. This concept is called "Rollovers as Business Startups" (ROBS) and allows retirement funds to be used without paying

---

[3] Should You Finance Your Business with a Home Equity Loan? – Gina Pogol; *clark.com*, January 19, 2016

taxes on the withdrawn funds or getting hit with an early withdrawal penalty

However, this can ultimately be a risky strategy, as you are putting 100% of your retirement funds into a single investment. In addition, the transaction itself is very complex and can be expensive requiring a special advisor to execute. Finally, this approach receives continuing oversight from the IRS to ensure all core elements are in compliance.

Benefits

- *No Debt, No Interest* – Investment is made as equity into business so no need to repay

- *Faster Access* – No credit check or time consuming underwriting process

- *Independence* – Avoid bringing in additional investors thus retaining 100% ownership

Challenges

- *Initial Setup* – Requires establishing a special structure (e.g. a C-corporation) to own and operate the business plus setting up a 401(k) Profit Sharing Plan

- *Significant Compliance* – Ongoing plan maintenance requires filing annual reports and communicating the plan to new employees

- *Retirement Fund Risk* – Place future retirement savings at peril as capital is invested in new business

IV. **Crowd Funding** – *Let's pitch this "baby" on-line for the world to see!*

A hot trend for raising money through the web from a large group of individuals is rewards based crowd funding. This approach offers your team an alternative to traditional small-business financing and provides the means to transform promising ideas into a profitable reality — without having to pay back a penny.

It starts by you crafting a compelling story about your brewery project or brew pub idea and securing pledges of support in small amounts (e.g. $25). A craft brewer will provide an low-cost incentive (e.g. t-shirt or logo glass) in return for donations

This approach allows your team to launch exciting new ideas at minimal risk without the burden of repaying a loan. The process uses websites such as Kickstarter, Indiegogo, GoFundMe and Crowdrise.[4]

Benefits

- Low Cost - This is one of the least costly ways to raise capital. Fees are a percentage of the money raised, and businesses may select rewards that let them keep the bulk of each donation.

---

[4] Rewards-Based Crowd funding: What It Is, When It Works – Jackie Zimmermann; *nerdwallet.com,* December 6, 2017

- *Easy to Do* - No collateral, credit check or previous experience is needed and no ownership is lost

- *Brand Awareness* – The exposure gained on the funding websites establishes a customer base, brand loyalty and feedback on new products.

Challenges

- *Project Size* – Typically not appropriate for businesses requiring funding beyond about $100,000 or showcasing complex ideas.

- *Competitive Exposure* – Pitching your vision on line risks having it stolen by anyone else unless you have patents or other protections.

- *Goal Requirements* – Unless you reach a specified target that funds raised may have to be forfeited.

V. **SBA Loans** – *Oh my goodness the government can actually help with money!*

    The good news is that once your team establishes a positive "track record" many more financing options become available. This typically entails being in business more than a year and having a good credit history.[5]

    No doubt, Small Business Administration (SBA) loans are one of the most attractive solutions to finance your brewery's expansion. SBA loans are guaranteed by the federal government, which allows lenders to offer

---

[5] How to Start a Craft Brewery – Tony Armstrong; *nerdwallet.com*, March 11, 2016

them with flexible terms and low rates. In fact, securing one can help you grow your business without taking on possibly crippling debt.[6]

However, there is one significant drawback: It can be time consuming and rigorous to get a loan from the SBA. The SBA's requirements are stringent, and applicants must also meet the underwriting criteria of the bank providing the money. Hence, you may hear that some entrepreneurs will skip this approach after becoming disillusioned over extra paperwork and long decision periods.

Benefits

- *Lower Interest Cost* – Since the loan is backed by government the interest rate is typically lower than other business loans.

- *More Repayment Time* – Depending on the use for loan proceeds you will have between 7 years (working capital) and 25 years (real estate) to repay.

- *Independence* – Can provide a useful option to selling off more of your equity as the brewer grows and stabilizes its operations.

Challenges

- *Personal Guarantees* – Often requires the pledge of your home or other significant asset as collateral to ensure you have "skin" in the business.

---

[6] SBA Loans: What You Need to Know – Andrew Wang; *nerdwallet.com*, December 19, 2017

- *Approval Period* – It takes longer to be approved and is a more invasive process than previous funding options.

- *Retirement Fund Risk* – Place future retirement savings at peril as capital is invested in new business.

VI. **<u>Conventional Bank Loans</u>** – *Will my local community banker help launch my brewery dreams!*

A place that a lot of entrepreneurs like your self will look for funds is a traditional bank. This can be a local community-based bank, regional specialty craft lender or a large national financial institution.

The product is issued in the form of debt that generally carries a specific interest rate and pre-set repayment period. This financing option can often be structured using either variable-rate (e.g. payment changes periodically) or fixed-rate (e.g. payment stays flat) alternatives plus flexible down payment.

Your team can use the funding obtained for brewery expansion, other loan refinancing, equipment purchases, working capital, construction and more. A key goal for your team is selecting a "product" that allows you the most flexibility in when you must start repayment.

Some banks will allow you to pay "interest only" for the first few years as your

148

brewery gets established. This can help avoid experiencing a "burn rate " (e.g. more expenses than income) that will keep you awake at night wondering how to make ends meet.

In general, most banks will require a significant asset as collateral (e.g. brewery equipment, revenue or cash flow) to make the loan less risky for the lender.

Benefits

- *Customized Terms* – Can be structured with flexible down payment and repayment options to match brewery's growth plan

- *Competitive Rates* – Will provide a sliding scale of interest rates depending on the credit worthiness and operating success of your business.

- *More Repayment Time* – Depending on the use for loan proceeds you will have between 7 years (working capital) and 25 years (real estate) to repay.

Challenges

- *Personal Guarantees* – Often requires the pledge of your home or other significant asset as collateral to ensure you have "skin in the game".

- *Stringent Requirements* – Applicants must satisfy the strict underwriting criteria of the lending group.

- *Approval Period* – It takes longer to be approved and is a more invasive process than previous funding options.

A debt investment in a craft brewery is typically a term loan; at some point, the investors who financed the debt are no longer involved and the founders of the business own 100% of the company. Equity fundraising provides investors with downside risk that is similar to that of a debt investment (i.e. the business goes bankrupt and never returns any capital or interest), but also provides the ability for investors to share in the upside potential of the business. Depending on the terms of the offering, equity investors can even receive guaranteed dividends and the first right to any capital returned through a bankruptcy filing or liquidation.

There are multiple sources of equity capital. Venture Capital (VC) firms are certainly an option, although they are often focused on high-growth sectors like biotechnology and software. Receiving an equity investment from a VC often requires extremely investor-friendly terms, including multiple Board Seats and, potentially, a degree of control over the everyday operation of the business.

High net worth individuals are another source of capital. These investors are often interested in a project for personal reasons (a "vanity" investment) and don't have the time or energy to demand oversight of day-to-day operations.

They are typically savvy, though, and as a result will drive a hard bargain when the terms of the deal are debated. In the past, finding individuals with enough net worth to consider such an investment was very challenging.

VII. **<u>Angel Investors</u>** – *I will sing praises to your generosity if you help fund my craft brewery dreams!*

Your first level of real equity capital is often sourced from individuals referred to as "Angel" investors that invest in exciting startups or individual teams. The term first originated with Broadway, when wealthy individuals gave money to propel theatrical productions.

You may find this group among your friends and family who have more capital to assist your brewery as it grows. These individuals can provide a one-time investment to help "jump start" your business or offer an ongoing source of money to carry through anticipated "growing pains".

In general, Angel investors will provide you with more favorable terms compared with other lenders, since they usually invest in the entrepreneur starting the business rather than the viability of the business. Angel investors are focused on helping startups take their first steps, rather than the possible profit they may get from the business[7].

<u>Benefits</u>

---

[7] Angel Investor – Definition; investopedia.com

- *Silent Partners* – Individuals are often interested in a project for personal reasons (e.g. I love beer) and thus don't demand oversight of day-to-day operations

- *Lower Cost* – Investors willing to forgo higher interest rates for being part of an exciting and relatable business

- *Fill the Gap* – Provides funding for entrepreneurs who are still financially struggling through start up and not eligible for traditional bank financing.

Challenges

- *Sharing Ownership* – Typically must surrender a portion of your ownership stake in exchange for a capital influx.

- *Enhanced Monitoring* – Requires advanced documentation to remain in compliance with SEC (Security & Exchange Commission) regulations.

- *Strict Regulations* – These investors must be "accredited" having net worth exceeding $1million and annual income of $200,000 or more.

VIII. **Private Equity/Venture Capital Firms** – *Watch out, the sharks are swimming around you looking for a tasty meal!*

Once your brewery is well established and experiencing accelerated revenue and volume growth new equity capital options become available. Venture Capital (VC) is especially useful if your growth strategy to reach a regional brewery size includes acquisitions and/or strategic partnerships.

However, these privately held firms often are interested in high-growth sectors (e.g. software and

152

biotechnology) where they can earn a 20% plus return on their investment. These firms understand the downside risk (e.g. the business goes bankrupt and no one gets paid) yet also recognize the unique growth potential with craft beer investments (e.g. share in the upside potential business).

Depending on the terms of the offering, equity investors can even receive guaranteed dividends and the first right to any capital returned through a bankruptcy filing or liquidation. Thus, your team should carefully consider the "fit" you have this potential capital source on pursuing a long-term strategy for the brewery.

Benefits

- *Capacity Building* – These professional organizations can provide valuable resources of time, treasure and experience to rapidly grow your business.

- *Capital Influx* – May offer a significant increase in cash resources to ensure your long-term vision is not hindered due to insufficient funding sources.

- *Exit Strategy* – Can provide the opportunity for your founders group to "cash out" of the business through a strategic acquisition or joint venture with another brewer.

Challenges

- *Significant Documentation* – Private equity placements require a detailed bundle of legal documents and careful consideration by all parties.

- *Big Equity Stake* – These significant cash contributions typically come at a high cost (e.g. over 35% of outstanding stock)

- *Active Involvement* – VC's often require extremely investor-friendly terms, including multiple Board seats, and potential control over daily operations.

What are other Strategic Options for my Brewery?

You will find that some brewers are seeking partnerships with other like-minded entities rather than going it alone. This "craft-on-craft" deal strategy allows smaller breweries to often combine their distribution networks and sales forces. This was the case when Green Flashing Brewing Co., of San Diego, purchased Alpine Beer Co. Company. The founders were seeking a "new company" structure post acquisition that resulted in a merged distribution system but with separate beer brands.

Though this M&A strategy can create some conflicts should breweries be sharing the same markets, the consolidation among entrepreneurial breweries can benefit both companies in terms of market awareness, brewing efficiencies, and shared resources. It is interesting to see this sort of M&A activity, which brings together relatively equal partners that are largely committed to the ideals of craft beer.

You may also find another popular strategy in the "craft beer space" is the Employee Stock Ownership Plan, (e.g. ESOP). This approach is especially beneficial for founders that want to reward their employees, especially those that have been with the brewery for a long time.

Ultimately, it provides your team with a path for employees to be vested in the company, plus existing shareholders can receive some desired liquidity. ESOPs are a tax efficient way for owners to realize a return on their privately held business while providing wealth-generating opportunities to their employees[8].

Under the ESOP agreement, you establish a trust that acquires shares from the existing shareholders, typically using a company guaranteed bank loan. Then shares are granted to the employees who "vest" over a pre-determined time frame.

Going forward, the craft beer industry will most likely continue its robust growth due to the significant momentum occurring both domestically and overseas. Presently, there are over 6,000 brew pubs, microbreweries and regional breweries in the US, the most in history.

Nevertheless, despite these high numbers, the craft beer industry continues to rapidly expand, although now at a slower rate. Thus, your team can indeed find a brewery operating strategy that will be profitable across any type of business model. This is primarily due to the

---

[8] Popular craft beer capital strategies: Considerations to manage expansion, grow distribution and maintain profitability – Brian Mulvaney; *craftbrewingbusiness.com,* August 24, 2015

insatiable thirst of craft beer drinkers for the "latest and greatest" innovative quaffs and tasting room experiences.

Finally, as your brewery looks to expand its operations, you must focus on how a capital strategy aligns with the overall business strategy. In fact, understanding the unique motivations of all the various capital providers outlined above, craft brewers can secure money and execute their growth strategies for greater long-term success.

Book Summary

This final chapter of Occupation Fermentation briefly recaps all the most important elements highlighted in the book.

How do you get started in the craft beer business? What are the lessons learned for starting your own brewery or expanding an existing enterprise? I offer four key insights about running a profitable craft brewing business as takeaways from this book.

First, it is imperative that you brew a really amazing tasting beer. It is not enough that you developed a product in your garage that your friends and neighbors rave about as being awesome. It is vital to receive outside validation before jumping head long into this very competitive business and buying a load of expensive equipment.

Second, it is important you create a fun and memorable brand that everyone easily recognizes. A critical element in building a successful craft brewery is the ability to consistently connect with your primary audience. This can be the local folk that stop by your tasting room on a Friday evening for a quick pint or those beer geeks that chase award-winning drafts throughout the country. No matter their age or stage in life it helps to have a hook that draws people to your doors.

Third, it is vital that your dedicated customers help spread the word among their friends and colleagues. It also is important to establish a dedicated following for your brewery where customers and guests will visit for a tour, taste your innovative brews and also take home attractive branded merchandise. These brand ambassadors will help spread the word of your amazing beer near and far.

Fourth, you must earn a significant financial return for all your hard work. The ultimate goal it to not only have a ball in the craft beer business but also make money. This is a capital-intensive business and you will need to tap a variety of resources for both start-up and expansion investments. The individuals, groups, banks, finance companies, angel investors and private equity firms all have different motivations in backing your specific enterprise. Whether they are beer lovers, think it is totally cool to be an owner of a craft brewery or are a large conglomerate, investors want a return on their money in a reasonable timeframe (less than five years)!

What Do I Need to Know?

Becoming a craft brewery entrepreneur raises a whole list of questions that need to be answered. For instance: What do I name my brewery and who is my core customer? How much space will I need and what type of equipment? What style of beer and how much volume should I expect to make and sell my first few years in the business? What will be the impact of changing consumer tastes for IPAs versus other styles of beer? How effectively do I need my facility to run in order to be cost efficient and make money? How will I get my product into stores and restaurants for sale? What type of merchandise should I sell to promote my brewery?

Determining the ideal targeted strategy for engaging customers can help your team gain traction in the local marketplace for expanding your business in the six following ways:

- *Build and grow your reputation*
- *Stand apart from competitors*
- *Convey stability*
- *Positively influence potential customer's purchasing decisions*
- *Acquire new customers easier*
- *Construct loyalty and trust*

Your company's brand name is more than just its logo, instead it serves a greater purpose highlighting what image your brewery projects outwardly to the community. It clearly shows both potential clients and consumers the experience they will receive with friends and family when enjoying your product.

The ability to manage your brew team and operate at 85% efficiency (or better) will help determine how quickly your operation will be profitable. Utilizing a larger brewhouse will help drive down the cost per ounce to produce your beer and help maintain improved quality.

Plus it requires an equal amount of time to produce a smaller (3barrel), or larger (30 barrel), batch of your great beer with your equipment size being the deciding factor.

Finally, your team's ability to properly forecast marketplace demand and match it against production schedules will determine whether your enterprise succeeds or fails! Ultimately you must assess how productive your brewery team is at wringing a high yield from each batch of lager, stout or IPA brewed.

What Makes a Craft Beer?

Plainly stated, craft beer is a malt beverage that is not brewed by one of the big "mega-brewery" corporations such as AB/In-Bev or MolsonCoors. The Brewer's Association defines craft beer as a product created by a brewer that is small, independent, and traditional.

These groundbreaking brew masters demand high quality and often expensive ingredients that enhance the flavor and character of their latest creations. The length and nature of your fermentation process can change dramatically with the style of beer being produced.

How to Achieve A Strong Brand Presence

Brand presence and awareness is often measured by how well a consumer can identify and connect with both your brand and company. Here are some key strategies your team may want to utilize in creating a stronger brand presence.

First, focus on your target audience. Create a personal connection between your brand and the craft beer drinker. Maintaining impeccable customer service and speaking to your audience in a way they will respond to, not just the way you want to say something, can help this level of trust grow.

Second, remain consistent with the image you created for your brewery or brew pub operation. How you present your brand should be clear across all channels and to everyone that encounters your line of unique and innovative craft beers. Your branding should be integrated into every aspect of the brewery's marketing toolkit including website, social media, advertising, point of sale flyers and other merchandise thus maintaining a strong tie-in that is easily understood.

Third, brewery themed merchandise is another opportunity to both reinforce the overall brand messaging and increase your cash flow. The value of having true believers out in the marketplace freely advertising your products is invaluable for building a stable business. There is also the benefit of having customers and visitors take home high margin souvenirs after visiting your tasting room.

Finally, whether your new enterprise is based on a city, animal, plant, mythical creature, family name, embarrassing incident or other idea you now will need to make sure your new brand name is properly protected. A critical issue that is frequently overlooked by both new and experienced brewers is securing federal trademark registration.

What is Your Success Plan?

Year after year craft beer fans keep demanding new and varied tastes from their favorite brewery. Craft brewers around the country are challenged to build new facilities that expand brewing capacity, distribute in new markets and increase innovation to meet this evolving demand.

This means that new investment and funding opportunities are suddenly available that previously did not exist as investors become even more enamored with this industry segment.

The available investment options vary widely. Thanks to the rapidly expanding love affair between consumers and craft brewers more Initial Public Offerings (IPO) and Merger & Acquisition (M&A) deals will continue in this industry.

You will quickly discover that once your brewery is fully operational and expands its revenue or volume, the existing processes and procedures often must be changed for greater efficiency. Simultaneously, you are going to find that beer connoisseurs expect continuous innovation in the craft segment. Thus you and your team must work even more diligently to maintain and grow customer loyalty with new, diverse and tasty product introductions.

Here are some key questions to consider among your team and potential funders.

- Should you borrow money or have interested parties become owners?
- How are your long-term desires and expectations matched with outside investors?
- Will you be able to pay back a loan during the lean years following startup?
- What is the real cost of the capital and can it be reduced as the business grows?
- If there are equity partners, are they expecting cash and when?
- What is the exit strategy for you and your investors to ultimately cash out?

Different types of equity, angel or institutional investors have varying expectations for financial return. You will discover angel or equity investors expect higher returns on their investment in exchange for their perceived risk in supporting your craft business. Institutions are sophisticated entities that are now investing in craft brewers to provide growth capital and acquisition platforms. These returns can come as distributions to shareholders, as buyouts by other investors or through the sale of the company.

You will find that some brewers are seeking partnerships with other like-minded entities rather than going it alone. This craft-on-craft deal strategy allows smaller breweries to often combine their distribution networks and sales forces.

Though this M&A strategy can create some conflicts if breweries share the same markets, the consolidation among entrepreneurial breweries can benefit both companies in terms of market awareness, brewing efficiencies and shared resources.

Consider these exit strategies. Do you want to become a large regional brewery? How long will you stay active in the brewery? Will you consider a sale to one of the Big Beer conglomerates? These and more questions are worth considering to ensure that all of your partners and team members are fully aligned with the future vision of your business.

In Summation

Perhaps you started this journey as a home brewer tinkering with that special Juicy IPA recipe in the early morning hours in your garage. It could be you just enjoy a cold Coffee Porter of Scottish Ale and found the best beer in town at your local brew pub. Alternatively, you may have jumped into this expanding industry with a few buddies buying an existing micro-brewery that needed your special skill set and marketing touch. No matter your path, understanding the underlying motivation will make the days of blood, sweat and tears all worthwhile!

A great way to figure out your end game is to have a clear set of goals from the very beginning. **Occupation Fermentation** is all about taking your passion and enthusiasm for craft beer and convert it into a profitable enterprise. This book offers a practical roadmap to success, for newcomers to experts, based upon real-life stories and experiences from prosperous brewers of all sizes

Ultimately, you must decide what matters the most in building a successful craft beer business. There are numerous ways to measure your accomplishments that should be considered. A few sample questions to reflect upon include:

- Should your brewery be known primarily for its award-winning brews?
- How important is earning a significant return on your investment of time and treasure?
- Does your team want to be a positive voice enhancing your local community?
- How long do you want to stay actively engaged in your brew pub or craft brewery?
- What size operation do you aspire to become (e.g. Regional or National distribution)?

- Will you consider selling your enterprise to a "Big Beer" conglomerate?

Finally, there are numerous ways to cash out of the business. Whether through a brewery sale, joint venture, public offering or acquisition by another larger entity. No matter which approach you choose it is imperative that your financial partners and team members are fully aligned with the future vision for the business.

<u>What Is the Next Step?</u>

It may indeed be your vision and life mission to undertake Occupation Fermentation! **Today is the time to jump into this exciting and dynamic industry and for you to have a blast living the craft life!**

Thanks for joining me on this adventure into the exciting craft brewing industry!

I would be pleased to assist you and your team! I am available, on a consulting basis, to help craft brewers enhance their branding, marketing, operations and financial performance, **so please reach out for a free 30 minute exploratory call.**

I can be reached as follows:

Curtis C. Battles
Chief Advisor/CEO
Craft Beer Insights
60 North Meadows Lane
Stamford, CT 06903
Office: 203.461.8711
Cell: 203.918.7780
E-Mail: craftbeerinsights@gmail.com
Website: www.craftbeerinsights.com

Glossary

Essential Craft Beer Terminology

So your craft brewing vision is quickly moving forward. Whether you began as a home brewer, started a new brewpub or acquired an existing brewery there are a list of terms that go hand in hand with this growing industry. I anticipate that you may already be familiar with the majority of these items; however, it always helps to have an easily accessible resource for friends and potential investors looking to follow your dreams.

I have broken down this list into key categories that will likely be of interest to you. Please feel free to reference this whenever you encounter an unfamiliar word or concept in **Occupation Fermentation.** Many thanks to various brewers and bloggers [42] for providing the answers to key questions that popped into my head while researching the book.

The Basic Ingredients of Craft Beer

There are four basic ingredients used to make beer: malt, hops, yeast and water. Depending on the style of the beer, other ingredients such as grains or even fruits and spices may be added. These are the basics.

Malt: The base grain for all beer, malt is almost always made from barley. (However, wheat is used in addition to barley for particular styles of beer such hefeweizen or wheat beer.) Malt is created by soaking barley in water and then allowing it to germinate before drying and kilning it. This process enables the production of enzymes, which, during the brewing process, will convert starch into fermentable sugar. The kilning process

---

[42] David Jepsen, For Beer Lovers Only: A Craft Beer Glossary, Menusim.com, 12.12.2011

168

can also result in malt with characteristics that impart different flavors and colors in the final product.

Adjuncts: Other un-malted grains or sugars that are added to a beer to create different flavors or colors. Some examples are oats, rye, wheat, rice and corn. Honey and other sugars also fall into this category.

Hops: A green climbing vine that produces a flower in the shape of a green cone. After being harvested, the cones are dried and then used to make beer, lending bitterness and aroma. The aroma differs by variety. Popular varieties of hops in craft beer include:

- Cascade
- Centennial
- Amarillo
- Chinook
- Saaz
- Northern Brewer
- Willamette
- Mt. Hood
- Goldings
- Tettnang
- Fuggles
- Hallertau

Alpha acids: The main bittering agent in hops.

Ale Yeast: A top-fermenting yeast used to make ales. Ale yeast ferments at warmer temperatures (close to room temperature). The many varieties of ale yeast used for different flavors and aromas make it popular among craft brewers.

Lager Yeast: A bottom-fermenting yeast used to make lager-style beer. Lager yeast ferments best at lower temperatures, such as cellar temperatures that range from 40° to 50° F.

Brettanomyces (aka "Brett") and wild yeast: A special yeast used to make sour or wild beer. Usually, brewers and winemakers try to prevent this yeast from getting into the beer. However, barrel-aged and sour ales almost always have Brett or another "wild" yeast strain in order to produce the acidity and funky aromas.

Grist: The combination of different milled grains in a beer's composition.

Craft Beer by the Numbers

If you look at the label on a can or bottle of beer you'll see that the brewery has listed the ingredients as well as some numbers about the contents. While some of these terms might seem cryptic here is a brief idea of their meaning.

ABV: Alcohol by volume. This is a measurement of the amount of alcohol in the beer.

Gravity: The amount of sugar in the beer (or wine for that matter). Original gravity is that measurement before the beer has been fermented. Final gravity is the measurement after fermentation. The alcohol content of the beer can be calculated using the original and final gravities.

Plato: A measurement of original gravity. This term is used in both the wine and beer worlds.

IBU: International bittering units. Although sensitivity to bitterness will vary from person to person, this is an objective measure of the bitterness of a beer. This number is based on the amount of a natural resin (known as "alpha acids") in the hops, how much hops are used, and when the hops are added to the beer.

Making Craft Beer

Some breweries will use beer-making terminology to describe certain aspects of their beer. They might even use that terminology in the name of the beer itself. Here's what those terms mean.

170

Mash: A product of the brewing process, mash is what occurs when the malt and adjunct grains are steeped in water at a specific temperature, usually around 150° F or more. Steeping the grains activates the enzymes in the malt, which in turn converts the starch in the grains to sugars, a majority of which will be fermented by the yeast.

Wort: The sugary solution that is collected from the mash and then boiled. Beer is called "wort" until it has been fermented, at which point it becomes beer.

Boil: A step in the brewing process when the wort is boiled and hops are added to the brew. Boiling removes certain compounds from the wort, stops the enzymes that were activated during the mash, and sterilizes the wort. The boil typically lasts 60 minutes but can be longer depending on the brewer.

Bittering hops: Hops that are added to the beginning of the boil, resulting in more bitterness and less aroma in the final product.

Aroma hops: Hops that are added at the end of the boil, producing less bitterness and more aroma in the final product.

Dry-hopped: Refers to the addition of hops after the boil, during transfer to the fermenter, in the fermenter itself, or even after fermentation. This technique adds a lot of hop aroma without adding much more bitterness to the beer.

Wet-hopped (aka "fresh-hopped"): Normally hops are dried before being used to make beer. Wet-hopped beer uses hops that have been freshly harvested and not dried, producing unique flavors and aromas. These beers are produced after the hop harvest in August and September and are usually ready by late September or early October. Drink your wet-hopped beer as fresh as possible.

Fermentation: After the boil, the wort is cooled and transferred to a sterile fermenter, where yeast is added. Yeast eats the fermentable sugars and produces alcohol and carbon dioxide, thus fermenting the beer. Different varieties of yeast can result in different flavors in the beer. A beer made with a Belgian strain of yeast is much different than one made with a Californian strain of yeast.

Conditioning: The process of maturing and carbonating the beer. It is the last step before the beer is ready to drink. Carbonation can be added through natural conditioning in the bottle, cask or conditioning tank. Beer can also be force-carbonated.

Lightstruck: Also referred to as "skunked," lightstruck beer happens when hops are exposed to the sun. Clear or green bottles are much more susceptible.

Oxidation: As beer ages, it runs the risk of being exposed to oxygen. This is generally undesirable but in barley wines and stouts, oxidation can actually play an important part in flavor development.

Bottle-conditioned: Yeast is left in the bottle to induce further development over time, known beer changes, more complex flavors and aromas form.

Fobbing: When beer foams during production, bottling or on draught. Fobbing can also refer the presence of foam is actually causing significant loss of beer. This is however a positive thing in a bottle, providing a tighter seal once capped.

Drinking Craft Beer

Beer geeks use a lot of ways to describe the beer they drink. The following are some common beer descriptors that you might hear a fan use.

Hoppy: A beer that strongly exhibits the flavor and aroma of hops. Since hops can have many different flavors and aromas, it's hard to pinpoint exactly what somebody means by "hoppy." Typically, the beer is bitter and smells like citrus, pine resin or flowers. Other popular hop aromas include herbal or earthy.

Malty: A beer that strongly exhibits the qualities of the malt. The flavors and aromas of a malty beer may be described as grainy, barley-like, syrupy, roasty, fresh sweet toasty bread, and cooked sugar. Maltiness is not a measure of the sweetness of a beer because many malty pilsners are not sweet. A beer can be both hoppy and malty.

Head Retention: The foam that rests on top of the beer after it has been served. Retention is how long the head lasts in your glass. The head will exhibit aroma attributes of the beer that are not found after the head has died down. For this reason, as well as aesthetic and stylistic reasons, a beer with a good long-lasting head is desirable. Although a vast majority of beer styles call for good head retention, it is not the case for all beer styles.

Mouth feel: How the beer feels in your mouth. It can range from thin and watery to thick and silky. Most beers are somewhere in between.

Imperial: Beers that are described as "imperial" or "double" are larger versions of the style listed on the beer—not in volume, but in certain characteristics. For example, imperial beers usually have more malt, more alcohol, more sweetness, more bitterness and/or more hops.

Session: The basic idea of a session beer is that you can drink multiples of these beers over the course of an evening without falling off your stool. Some people are adamant that a session beer must have no more than 4% alcohol by volume, but the term is somewhat relative. A session beer could almost be considered the opposite of an imperial.

White Whale: This refers to the rarest, most delicious, hard-to-get beer. Theses are brews that have legendary stories written about them. A beer that, once sampled, is believed to change the life of the drinker forever.

Beer Vessels

Beer is served from a variety of vessels. The bottle is the most common but even certain types of bottles have their own names. Here is a list of containers you may encounter in your enterprise.

Bomber: A 22-ounce bottle of beer.

Cask (aka firkin): A barrel-shaped vessel for both conditioning and serving ale. The beer is placed in this vessel, stored at cellar temperatures (48-56°F), natural carbonation conditions the beer, and then the beer is served at cellar or room temperature (cellar temps are preferred). Casks are either connected to a special tap called a beer engine, or are served directly from a spigot in the cask.

Keg: A large vessel for serving beer on draft. Kegs come in many shapes and sizes. The typical keg is a ½ barrel or 15.5 gallons. A pony keg is 1/4 barrel or 7.75 gallons. A corny keg or log is 5 gallons or 1/6 barrel. One gallon of beer yields ten and a half 12 oz. servings.

Can: Large breweries have been using cans for years but craft beer in a can is a recent development. Cans never impart a metallic flavor because all cans are lined with plastic so that the beer never touches metal until you pour it out. Cans are great for beer because the beer is never exposed to light, and cans are more airtight than bottles, preventing oxidation.

Growler: A big glass jug (64 oz.) used to hold beer. Most brewpubs will allow you to buy and refill a growler.

Bung: Can refer both to the hole and the cylindrical stopper in a cask, keg or barrel.

Coolship: A large shallow container used to cool wort (the liquid containing grain sugars yielded outside temperature and wild yeast. The beer is then transferred to barrels for fermentation. Traditionally by many U.S. breweries as a more natural way of creating beer.

Carboy (also **demijohn**, or **jimmyjohn):** A rigid clear glass or plastic container commonly used for homebrewing. Each container holds a typical capacity of 20 to 60 litres (5 to 16 US gal). Carboys are primarily used for transporting liquids, often water or chemicals.

REFERENCES

Chapter One - Why Do You Want to Own a Brewery?

1. **Brainy Quotes: Maya Angelou** - *brainyquote.com*

2. **The U.S. Now Has 27 Million Entrepreneurs -** Leigh Buchanan; *Inc.*, September 2, 2015

3. **Entrepreneurship Definition** - *BusinessDictionary.com*

4. **Entrepreneur Definition** - *merriam-webster.com*

Chapter Two - Origins of the Craft Brewing Industry

1. **Revised Craft Brewer Definition -** *Brewers Association*, (2014), Real Beer News, 20(3).

2. **The Audacity of Hops: The History of America's Craft Beer Revolution** Thomas Acitelli, Chicago Review Press, 2013

3. **A Brewer's Guide to Opening a Nano Brewery** - Woodske, D.; *Self-published*, 2012

4. **Working Definition of Craft Beer** - Eddings, B.; thespruce.com, 2017

5. **Craft Beer in the United States: History, Numbers, and Geography** - Kenneth G. Elzinga, Carol Horton Tremblay and Victor J. Tremblay; *Journal of Wine Economics*, Volume 10, Number 3, 2015, Pages 242–274

6. **Beer Industry Update** – Annual, Beer Marketer's Insights

7. **The American Beer Story** – *Craftbeer.com*

Chapter Three - How Do You Make Great Beer?

1. **Brewing Process** - *Craft Brewers Guild; craftbrewersguildma.com*

Chapter Four - How Large Should I Build My Brewery?

1. **Number of Breweries -** *Brewers Association;* *brewersassociation.com*

2. **Brewery System Sizing Overview** – *Specific Mechanical Systems Ltd.;* specificmechanical.com

Chapter Five - What is the History of Beer Regulation?

1. **Al Capone** – Biography; biography.com

2. **SA Eliot Ness, a Legacy ATF Agent** – Bureau of Alcohol, Tobacco, Firearms and Explosives (ATF); atf.gov

3. **Government Beer Regulations** – Apex Publishers; *beer-brewing.com*, Chapter 22

4. **Seasonal Beer Management Best Practices for Distributors** – *Brewers Association;* *brewersassociation.com*

5. **Prohibition in the United States** – *Wikipedia; Wikipedia.com*

6. **What is a Beer Distributor?** – *National Beer Wholesalers Association; nbwa.org*

7. **AB/InBev finalizes $100B billion acquisition of SABMiller** – Lisa Brown; *chicagotribune.com*, October 11, 2016

Chapter Six - How do I Create a Brand and Market my Brewery?

1. **Benefits of a Strong Brand Presence and How to Achieve One** – Jaime Nacach; *Bloominari.com*, March 5, 2016

2. **9 Weird Brewery Names and the Stories Behind Them** – Danele Bova; *craftbeer.com*, January 24, 2017

brewery – Dave Clark; *entertainermag.com,* June 26, 2017

2. **Dos and Don'ts of Asking Family and Friends for Startup Funds?** – Tony Armstrong; *nerdwallet.com,* January 19, 2015

3. **Should You Finance Your Business with a Home Equity Loan?** – Gina Pogol; *clark.com,* January 19, 2016

4. **Rewards-Based Crowd funding: What It Is, When It Works** – Jackie Zimmermann; *nerdwallet.com,* December 6, 2017

5. **How to Start a Craft Brewery** – Tony Armstrong; *nerdwallet.com,* March 11, 2016

6. **SBA Loans: What You Need to Know** – Andrew Wang; *nerdwallet.com,* December 19, 2017

7. **Angel Investor** – Definition; investopedia.com

Popular craft beer capital strategies: Considerations to manage expansion, grow distribution and maintain profitability – Brian Mulvaney; *craftbrewingbusiness.com,* August 24, 2015

Curtis C. Battles

Author & Entrepreneur

Curt Battles is an author, strategist and management consultant in the rapidly evolving Craft Beer Industry. Having worked with Disney, Pepsi Cola, Lufthansa Sky Chefs and Guest Quarters hotels he developed an expertise in food and beverage operations.

He has a Bachelor of Science with Distinction from Cornell University. Curt also graduated with an MBA from Northwestern University's Kellogg Graduate School of Management.

He started his post-business school career with the Pepsi Cola Company. During his almost decade long-tenure he served in several positions of increasing responsibility including a Controller and as a Director of Strategic Planning.

Curt is currently a speaker and advisor to a broad range of entrepreneurial ventures. Most recently, he launched **Craft Beer Insights (**www.craftbeerinsights.com) to provide guidance on branding, operations and value creation to firms throughout the U.S.

Curt's outside interests include cooking, travel, cycling and photography. He and his wife Sheryl reside in Stamford (CT) with their daughter Kendall, plus two loving dogs, a yellow lab girl (Jazz) and a golden retriever boy (Ryder).

"Curt has the perfect background to provide a unique perspective on building a successful brewery. He brings a wealth of knowledge in real estate, craft beer operations, product development, branding, strategy and finance. Curt understands the many challenges facing entrepreneurs while also bringing practical advice. He is adept at supporting both start-ups and already existing breweries who may want to rethink strategy or make more money."

Gary Breitbart
Growth Company Advisor – Business Council of Fairfield County

"Working with Curt on this book was an amazing experience! When you get to know him you will discover his many layers of technical and disciplinary skill and insight, as I did, that can only help you grow in your understanding and knowledge of the craft beer business. Curt will surprise you at every turn by asking deep and then again even deeper questions to get to the bottom of the challenges you face in running your brewery. He will then offer alternative solutions using his creativity and knowledge, which he acquired during his over 40 years of success in both corporate and entrepreneurial roles in industry. He is all about finding the gold inside of a business, and making certain that his clients are profitable, while staying ahead of their competition, always charging forward at the cutting edge of their industry"

Richard Glover
Publisher – Penn-Glover Publishing

Curt Offers a ½ Hour FREE Consultation to any Brewery Owner or Prospective Brewery Owner and Offers Advice and Insights on Operations, Strategy, Marketing and Merchandising, Merger, Acquisition or Divestitures, and Raising Capital.

Please visit his website for contact information at: CraftBeerInsights.com

Made in the USA
Columbia, SC
07 December 2018